THE
LITTLE
BOOK
OF
WILTSHIRE

DEE LA VARDERA

First published 2013
Reprinted 2016

The History Press
The Mill, Brimscombe Port
Stroud, Gloucestershire, GL5 2QG
www.thehistorypress.co.uk

British Library Cataloguing in Publication Data.
A catalogue record for this book is available from the British Library.

ISBN 978 0 7524 6993 5

Typesetting and origination by The History Press
Printed in Turkey by Imak.

CONTENTS

	Acknowledgements	5
	Introduction	6
	What They Say About Wiltshire	7
1	The Wonders of Wiltshire	9
2	Record Breakers	25
3	Military Matters	38
4	Law & Order	52
5	Working Life	64
6	Leisure Time	80
7	Inventors, Pioneers & Scholars	95
8	Literary Wiltshire	109
9	Wiltshire's Nobel Laureate	124
10	Musical Wiltshire	129
11	Stage, Screen & TV	139
12	Film File	150
13	Animal Tales	155
14	On this Day	163
	Bibliography	191
	Illustrations	192

ACKNOWLEDGEMENTS

Thank you to everyone who helped me with my researches, with contributions and in verifying the material gathered. Most entries are the result of a combination of sources from original documents, archive material, newspapers, magazines, books, the internet and human memory.

Particular thanks to: Robert Goddard; David Waters, the Great Bustard Group; Peter Stowe, Castle Combe Circuit; Tony Pickernell, Garrison Theatre, Tidworth; Sarah Jane Kenyon, Dents Glove Museum; Simon Cook and Martin Macintyre, The Rifles (Berkshire and Wiltshire) Museum; Paul Connell, Chippenham Museum; Roger Frost, Market Lavington Museum; Kate Fieldon, Bowood House; David Dawson, Wiltshire Heritage Museum; Paul Gahan, Swindon Library; David Birk, Trowbridge Museum; Felicity Jones, STEAM Swindon; Steve Hobbs, Wiltshire and Swindon History Centre (WSHC); and John Rattray, Wiltshire Wildlife Trust. Thanks also to Norman Beale, Graham Carter, Barry Cooper, Gerry Hughes, Terry Gilligan and Mike Stone.

INTRODUCTION

The wonderful county of Wiltshire attracts millions of visitors from around the world every year – most, it seems, making their way to Stonehenge or Harry Potter's Hogwarts at Lacock or Longleat to see the lions. But there is so much else to see from Downs to Plain: white horses cut into chalk hillsides, canals and crop circles, fine architecture in churches, great houses and colleges, picturesque villages and hidden hamlets.

Farming and small businesses, new technology and commerce work side by side, keeping the county developing and changing as it always has over the centuries. Multiplexes and supermarkets have replaced breweries and mills. Our county records office, rated one of the best archive services in the country, stands where livestock were auctioned, in what was once the largest one-day cattle market in England.

But it's people who make a place. Wiltshire can boast a long line of wonderful men and women over the centuries, from poets to politicians, artists to archaeologists, singers to suffragettes who have left their legacy both here and abroad. This book is packed with them, along with the unsung heroes and heroines, oddballs and eccentrics, as well as quite a few rogues and villains.

Here are stories to celebrate and entertain, about the funny, the unusual and the obscure relating to our very own green and pleasant land – Wiltshire. Have a good read or just dip in as the fancy takes.

Dee La Vardera, 2013

WHAT THEY SAY ABOUT WILTSHIRE

'Welcome to Camillashire. For more than 30 years Camilla, the Duchess of Cornwall, has lived and loved in Wiltshire.' (*Daily Mail*, 20 August 2007)

People in Wiltshire are the fourth happiest in the country according to the Office of National Statistics Well-being Survey (2012)

'A fine Champion Country pleasant for all sports, Rideing, Hunting, Courseing, Setting and Shooteing.' (Celia Fiennes, *Through England on a Side Saddle in the Time of William and Mary*, 1695)

'The Chicago of the Western Counties.' (Richard Jefferies, on New Swindon, 1867)

'Everywhere the same squat rows. It was like wandering through a town for dingy dolls.' (J.B. Priestley on New Town, Swindon, taken from *English Journey*, 1934)

'Wiltshire itself helps to supply London with cheese, bacon and malt, three very considerable articles, besides that vast manufacture of fine Spanish cloths … that it is thereby rendered one of the most important counties in England, that is to say, important to the public wealth of the kingdom.' (Daniel Defoe, *A Tour Through The Whole Island Of Great Britain*, 1724–1726)

'The hawthorn bushes were loaded with their sweet May snow, and in the glowing afternoon sun the sheets of buttercups stretched away under the bright elms like a sea of gold.' (Revd Francis Kilvert of Langley Burrell's diary, 17 May 1874)

'Wiltshire is without rival among English Counties for the extent and character of its antiquities. Its woodlands are charming. The valleys of its greater rivers have a detailed loveliness all their own, while thoroughly English in general effect.' (R.N. Worth, *Tourist's Guide To Wiltshire*, 1887)

The local population of North Wiltshire 'are phlegmatique, skins pale and livid, slow and dull, heavy of spirit ... they only milk the cowes and make cheese; they feed chiefly on milke meats, which cooles their braines too much, and hurts their inventions. These circumstances make them melancholy, contemplative, and malicious; by consequence whereof come more law suites out of North Wilts, at least double the Southern parts.' (John Aubrey, *The Natural History of Wiltshire*, 1656–1691)

'In the city of Salisbury doe reigne the dropsy, consumption, scurvy, gowte; it is an exceeding dampish place.' (John Aubrey)

'Swindon represents the eastern edge of the UK's largest silicon design cluster – twice the size of Cambridge, and second only to Silicon Valley itself.' (National Endowment for Science, Technology & the Arts (NESTA) Report 'Chips with everything' October 2010)

1

THE WONDERS OF WILTSHIRE

Stonehenge, Avebury, and Associated Sites were listed by UNESCO (1986) as World Heritage property of 'Outstanding Universal Value' and 'internationally important for its complexes of outstanding prehistoric monuments'.

STONEHENGE

Stonehenge covers 2,600 hectares and is 'the most architecturally sophisticated prehistoric stone circle in the world'. English Heritage describes it as 'a unique lintelled stone circle surrounded by landscape containing more than 350 burial mounds and major prehistoric monuments such as the Stonehenge Avenue, the Cursus, Woodhenge and Durrington Walls.' Latest carbon dating pinpoints its construction to 2,300 BC say Professors Tim Darvill and Geoff Wainwright. Its purpose: 'It is certain that Stonehenge was built as a temple to the sun and the changing seasons, carefully aligned to mark midsummer and midwinter', agrees Julian Richards.

Visitor Facts
1951 – 124,000 visitors
1971 – 550,000 visitors
1990 – 687,000 visitors
2010/11 – 1,023,000 visitors, of whom 50 per cent were from overseas
It regularly appears in top ten lists of most popular places to visit in Britain.

Who Owned Stonehenge?
Stonehenge was in private hands from the middle ages onwards, from the Benedictine nuns of Amesbury Abbey through to Henry VIII, who took the abbey and its land in 1540. He passed it down to various

families, including Edward Seymour, Earl of Hertford and the Marquess of Queensbury, then to the Antrobus family who bought the estate in 1824.

An attempt to sell Stonehenge in 1899 failed when there was public outcry and questions raised in Parliament. Sir Edmund Antrobus offered the 1,300 acres site, including 'certain pasturage and sporting rights' to the Government for £125,000. A *Punch* cartoon of 30 August 1899 speculated on what might happen to the site if Stonehenge were sold. In the end, Antrobus fenced off the site and imposed an admission charge of 1s to visitors. When the heir to the Antrobus baronetcy was killed in the First World War, the estate was finally put up for sale.

A SUGGESTION.

HOW STONEHENGE MIGHT BE POPULARISED IF THE GOVERNMENT BOUGHT IT.

Going, Going, Gone!

The last private owner of Stonehenge was Sir Cecil Herbert Edward Chubb, 1st Baronet (1876–1934) who was born in Shrewton, and attended Bishop Wordsworth's School, Salisbury and lived at Bemerton Lodge. He went to a Messrs Knight Frank and Rutley auction held in the Palace Theatre, Salisbury, on 21 September 1915 where he bought Lot 15 (Stonehenge, with 30 acres adjoining land) on a whim as a gift for his wife, paying £6,600. Chubb gave Stonehenge to the Government on 26 October 1918, handing it over to Sir Alfred Mond, First Commissioner of Works. Its current valuation is in the region of £51 million.

Trouble at the Stones

The first organised Free Festival at Stonehenge was held in June 1974 to celebrate the summer solstice and continued for eleven years. In 1985, Prime Minister Margaret Thatcher banned the solstice gathering and a High Court judge granted an order to enforce a

four–mile exclusion zone around the Stones. There were violent clashes between more than 1,000 police, many in riot gear, drawn from six counties and the MOD, and the convoy of several hundred new-age travellers, peace activists, anti-nuclear campaigners and free festival-goers en route to Stonehenge. There were 520 arrests in what became known as the 'Battle of the Beanfield', after the field where the convoy was camping.

SIX PHONEYHENGES

Stonehenge, Alton Park, Staffordshire, is a Grade II listed early nineteenth-century garden folly, described in the National Heritage List as 'massive stone blocks. 3 bays with 2-tier central bay, monumental lintels'. It was built by the 15th Earl of Shrewsbury in the gardens of his estate, now part of Alton Towers Amusement Park.

The Britton Celtic Cabinet, 1824, in the Wiltshire Heritage Museum, Devizes, was made for George Watson Taylor of Erlestoke Park, MP for Devizes (1826–1832). In the shape of a Stonehenge trilithon it is made from mahogany and pine with pollarded elms and bird's eye maple veneer with glass fronted panels displaying watercolour views of megalithic monuments. The glass cabinet on top contains a cork model of Stonehenge made by Henry Browne, and a model of Avebury in a drawer beneath.

Foamhenge, Natural Bridge, Virginia, USA. This was the fastest Stonehenge ever erected. Mark Cline, fibreglass artist, set up his exact replica made from styrofoam in a single day on 1 April, 2004. He carved 16 ft tall blocks of foam then anchored them in cement on his property, Enchanted Castle Studios in Natural Bridge, Virginia. It has become a popular attraction worldwide, much respected for its accuracy in appearance, layout and astronomical alignment.

Phonehenge, Myrtle Beach, South Carolina, USA. This half circle was created from a number of old–fashioned red British telephone boxes. It is used as performance area in the British Invasion section of the Freestyle Music Park, a 55–acre rock and roll themed amusement park near Myrtle Beach, opened in 2008. (Not to be confused with Phonehenge West (California) made from telephone poles by Alan Kimble Fahey, sentenced in December 2012 by a Los Angeles court to 565 days for failure to demolish his compound and structures).

Carhenge, Alliance, Nebraska, USA. Jim Reinders, farmer and artist, erected his homage to Stonehenge in 1987 built from 38 vintage American cars sprayed with grey paint. Over 80,000 tourists a year visit the site and it was voted No. 2 Wackiest Attraction in America in 2009.

Sacrilege, Turner Prize-winning artist Jeremy Deller's creation is a life-size replica of Stonehenge as a fully operational bouncy castle. It was launched in Glasgow in April and went on tour to twenty-five locations across Britain, as part of the London 2012 Cultural Olympiad.

AVEBURY

Avebury stone circle is the largest prehistoric stone circle in the world. It is fourteen times the size of Stonehenge and was built and altered over many centuries from about 2850 BC to 2200 BC. 'The encircling henge consists of a huge bank and ditch 1.3km in circumference, within which 180 local, unshaped standing stones formed the large outer and two inner circles.' (UNESCO) It is regarded by spiritual groups, such as druids, as an important spiritual centre and site for ritual.

On 15 June 1668, Samuel Pepys visited Avebury, and said of the area: 'Where, seeing great stones like those of Stonage standing up, I stopped, and took a countryman of that town, and he carried me and shewed me a place trenched in, like Old Sarum almost, with great stones pitched in it, some bigger than those at Stonage in figure, to my great admiration: and he told me that most people of learning, coming by, do come and view them, and that the King did so.'

Florrie's Ghost
The 400-year-old Red Lion Inn in the heart of the Avebury Circle appears in many top ten lists of most haunted places in Britain. One ghost said to haunt the pub is that of Florrie, killed by her husband who unexpectedly returned from the Civil War to find her with her lover. He shot the lover and slit his wife's throat, dragging her body to the well (still preserved in one of the pub's front rooms) where he threw it, sealing the well with a boulder.

How Marmalade Saved the Stones
Alexander Keiller (1889–1955) 'The Marmalade Millionaire' inherited the family business of James Keiller & Sons Dundee Marmalade when he was nine. He sold his shares in 1918 and used his wealth to pursue his many interests including racing cars, skiing, flying and archaeology. He became interested in Wiltshire with its Neolithic history and began buying land in 1924, including a large part of Windmill Hill, a mile north of Avebury. He added properties in the village, including the Manor House, and surrounding land with earthworks and stone circle. Thanks to his wealth, expertise and determination in excavating, recording and restoring the site, we are able enjoy its present-day splendour.

Two Special Stones
The Barber's Stone, re-erected by Keiller in 1938, was named after the skeleton discovered buried underneath the stone, along with a pair of scissors, a small iron lancet and three silver coins dating from early

fourteenth century. Thought to be a medieval barber-surgeon (or a tailor) who was crushed under a stone while helping locals to destroy and bury the stones, perhaps part of the attempts to rid the site of its pagan associations in response to pressure from the Church against such practices.

The Diamond or Swindon weighing 100 metric tonnes (the equivalent of two Chieftain tanks) is heavier than any stone at Stonehenge, and also one of the few megaliths that has never fallen or been moved.

SILBURY HILL

Silbury Hill is the largest prehistoric mound in Europe. Built around 2400 BC, it stands 39.5m high and comprises half a million tonnes of chalk. It is privately owned and managed by English Heritage. The purpose of this imposing monument still remains a mystery. It seems to have been all things to all people at one time or another. From a burial mound, a platform for astronomical observations to a place for druidical sacrifices or the motte of a castle. It has always been considered a place of spiritual significance, some believing it to be the omphalos or navel (the centre of the spiritual world), the sacred 'eye' or the pregnant earth goddess.

The King and the Snails
John Aubrey recorded an important visit to Silbury Hill in his *Natural History of Wiltshire* in 1663, 'I had the honour to waite on King Charles II and the Duke of York to the top of Silbury hill, his Royal Highnesse happened to cast his eye on some of these small snailes on the turfe of the hill. He was surprised by the novelty, and commanded me to pick some up, which I did about a dozen or more immediately; for they are in great abundance.'

Merry Making on the Mound
The *Bath Journal* for 7 September 1747 announced that: 'At King Cool's Theatre at Celbury-Hill (Silbury) near Marlborough (which is the most beautiful and magnificent mount in Europe) the 12th and 13th days of October, will be Bull-Baiting, Backsword Playing, Dancing, and other Divertions. The second day will be Wrestling, a Smock and Ribbons run for, and Foot-Ball Playing, eight of a Side. At this entertainment the Company of the Neighbouring Nobility, Members, Clergy, and the Rest of the King's Friends is desired; and as eleven years ago about Six Thousand People met at the said Hill, the Publick-Houses had not proper accommodation, therefore several Booths will be erected.'

TV's First Live Archaeological Dig
In 1968, David Attenborough, who was controller of BBC2 at the time, commissioned a dig of Silbury Hill led by Professor Richard Atkinson. This involved tunnelling into its depths to discover why it was there. At the time, the programme was judged a flop, since it found no treasure, no tomb and no real answers at all.

WEST KENNET LONG BARROW

This is 'the largest, most impressive and accessible Neolithic chambered tombs in Britain' and part of the Avebury World Heritage site. It was built around 3650 BC and briefly used as a burial chamber for fifty people before being blocked up. It was excavated in 1859 and in 1955-56. It is privately owned but looked after by English Heritage.

In the seventeenth century, Dr Troope from Marlborough is said to have stolen human bones from the Barrow to grind up and sell as a quack medicine.

It is said that at sunrise on Midsummer's Day, a white spectral figure appears, accompanied by a red-eared hound.

SALISBURY PLAIN

'The turfe is of a short sweet grasse, good for the sheep, and delightful to the eye, for its smoothnesse is like a bowling green, and pleasant to the traveller; who wants here only variety of objects to make his journey lesse tedious: for here is *nil nisi campus et aër*, not a tree, or rarely a bush to shelter one from a shower.' (John Aubrey, *The Natural History of Wiltshire*, 1656–1691)

Salisbury Plain is the largest area of chalk grassland in North-West Europe. Much of the land is designated as a Site of Special Scientific Interest (SSSI), Special Area Conservation (SAC) and Special Protection Area (SPA) for birds, and is rich in Scheduled Monuments (SM), as well as being the location of the Stonehenge World Heritage Site.

The Ministry of Defence has owned Salisbury Plain since 1897, when it began purchasing land, now totalling about 38,000 hectares (roughly the size of the Isle of Wight). This has enabled them to maintain this area as one of the best nature reserves in the country. Farmland has been carefully managed, and the absence of intensive farming methods has helped to create favourable conditions for all kinds of grasses and wild flowers to grow. This has helped to create a safe home for rare butterflies such as the Marsh Fritillary, Duke of Burgundy and Adonis Blue, and for birds such as Skylarks and summer visiting Stone Curlews, and now the Great Bustard. The regular movement of tanks across the land has proved useful too, for the rare Fairy Shrimp thrives in puddles in the tank tracks.

THE ROYAL HUNTING FOREST

Savernake Forest, near Marlborough, is the only privately owned forest in Britain and one of England's most important woodlands, being more than 1,000 years old. The forest ownership has an unbroken line from Norman times, passing down thirty-one generations – father to son (and four daughters) to the current hereditary warden, the Earl of Cardigan. The Grand Avenue of beech trees in Savernake was planted by Capability Brown in the 1790s, and runs for just under 4 miles across the 2,750 acres of woodland. One of the oldest trees in Britain is the Big Bellied Oak, aka the Decanter's Oak, on the side of the A346 road, south of Cadley. The forest is designated as an Area of Outstanding Beauty and a Site of Special Scientific Interest (SSSI) and managed by the Forestry Commission.

WINDMILL HILL

An important exhibit in the Alexander Keiller Museum, Avebury, is the Windmill Hill (Neolithic) Pot found during excavations at Windmill Hill, 'the classic Neolithic causewayed enclosure with three concentric but intermittent ditches', and part of the Avebury World Heritage Site. Archaeological excavations at the site in the 1920s revealed some of the earliest pots found in the British Isles. Pottery was first used in Britain at about the same time that farming was introduced from the Continent. This type of pottery was named after Windmill Hill because it was one of the first sites where it was recognised.

EIGHT WHITE HORSES

Westbury White Horse, aka Bratton Horse, is the largest and oldest of the eight horses carved into the chalk downland in Wiltshire. The present horse was cut in 1778.

Cherhill White Horse is the second largest and was cut in 1780.

Pewsey White Horse. The old horse was cut in 1785, the new one in 1937.

Marlborough White Horse, aka Preshute, was cut in 1804 and is maintained by Marlborough College.

Alton Barnes White Horse was cut on a hill known as Old Adam in
   1812 by Robert Pile, who is also said to have cut the Pewsey Horse
   (or possibly his father).
Hackpen White Horse, aka Winterbourne Bassett or Broad Hinton
   White Horse, was cut in 1838.
Broad Town was cut on downland outside the village around 1864.
Devizes Millennium is the newest one, cut in 1999.

THE RIDGEWAY

The Ridgeway National Trail is Britain's oldest road, possibly 5,000
years old or more, and is part of a much bigger track stretching 250
miles from the Dorset coast to the Wash in Norfolk. This surviving
part is 87 miles long and follows the ancient chalk ridge route used by
prehistoric man, probably travellers, herdsmen and soldiers. Sections
were also known as the 'herepath', Anglo-Saxon for 'army road'. The
road starts at Overton Hill near Avebury ending at Ivinghoe Beacon
in the Chiltern Hills.

SALISBURY CATHEDRAL

Salisbury Cathedral is one of the finest medieval cathedrals in Britain. It
took 38 years to build (AD 1220–1258) using: 60,000 tons of Chilmark
Stone; 10,000 tons of Purbeck Stone; 28,000 tons of oak for the roof,
and 420 tons of lead covering 4 acres used on the roof. It is dedicated
to the Blessed Virgin of the Assumption and was consecrated on
20 September 1258.

Claims to Fame
The tallest spire in Britain. At 404ft high it was completed in the
1330s. The top 30ft of tower and spire were rebuilt in 1945–51.

The largest cathedral close in Britain. Its shape is roughly a rectangle
measuring 80 acres. A licence to build a wall round the cathedral and
houses was granted by Edward III in 1327.

The largest secular cathedral cloisters in Britain. Unusual, as they were
never part of a monastic foundation and as Pevsner said, 'It was an
afterthought … It is entirely isolated from the cathedral.'

The world's oldest working clock. It has no face, only strikes the
hour, and can be found in the north nave aisle of the Cathedral. It

dates from AD 1386 and used to be situated in the Bell Tower, which was demolished in 1789.

The largest piece of modern art within a medieval cathedral. *The Salisbury Font*, designed by William Pye, was installed in the centre of the nave of the Cathedral and consecrated by the Archbishop of Canterbury on 28 September 2008. The reflections of the surrounding architecture and stained-glass windows in the still surface of the water in the vessel are particularly beautiful.

The first women Dean of a medieval cathedral. The Very Revd June Osborne, a former pupil of St Mary's School, Calne, took up post at the Cathedral in 2004.

MAGNA CARTA

'The greatest constitutional document of all times.'
Lord Denning, Master of the Roll, 1965

The Chapter House of Salisbury Cathedral holds the best preserved copy of only four remaining original copies of the 1215 Magna Carta. It was written on vellum (parchment made from calfskin) and measures 14 in x 17 in.

Clause 39 is one of the most famous from the document:

> No free man shall be seized or imprisoned, or stripped of his rights or possessions, or outlawed or exiled, or deprived of his standing in any other way, nor will we proceed with force against him, or send others to do so, except by the lawful judgement of his equals or by the laws of the land.

The British Library holds two copies and Lincoln Castle the other. The worldwide significance of Magna Carta was recognised in 2009, as it was inscribed in the UNESCO 'Memory of the World' register, which began in 1992 to protect and promote the world's documentary heritage through preservation and access.

SIX WINDOWS TO SEE

St Nicholas Church, Bromham
A memorial stained-glass window designed by William Morris in around 1870, which is dedicated to Irish poet Thomas Moore (1779–

1852) who was buried in the churchyard. Moore moved from Dublin in 1817 to Sloperton Cottage, Westbrook near Bromham.

Lacock Abbey
A lattice window, famous as the subject of the first camera negative picture taken by William Fox Talbot, who discovered the negative/positive photographic process in 1835.

St Michael's and All Saints' Church, Lyneham
Two stained-glass windows designed and made by Henry Haig of Shaftesbury, one commemorating the fiftieth anniversary of RAF Lyneham (1990); the other to mark the 47 Squadrons long association with Lyneham (2007).

Church of the Holy Cross, Seend
The Millennium Window, 2002, was designed and made by Andrew Taylor, FMGP, of Littleton Panell to celebrate past and present working life of the village. The lights of the window show aspects of agriculture, the woollen and weaving industry, iron ore mining and smelting, and the importance of the canal for transporting raw materials to and from the area.

Trinity Chapel, Salisbury Cathedral

The Prisoner of Conscience stained-glass window, 1980, was designed and cut by Gabriel Loire, of Chartres, from glass selected by his son, Jacques. The central lancet represents Christ as a prisoner of conscience of the first century; the outer lancets those of the twentieth century.

St Peter ad Vincula, Tollard Royal

The stained-glass window by Giuseppe Bernini of Milan was given as a memorial to the Honourable Alice Arbuthnot, daughter of George Pitt-Rivers, 4th Baron Rivers of Sudeley Castle, who was killed by lightning on her honeymoon in Switzerland while climbing the Schildhorn Alp on 21 June 1865.

SIX WORKS OF ART TO VIEW

The Annunciation (1463) by Fra Filippo Lippi in the Cabinet Room at Corsham Court, and Michelangelo's *Sleeping Cupid* (1496) is a must-see in the Octagon Room.

Glass Prism, etched glass by Laurence Whistler exhibited in Salisbury Cathedral is a memorial to his brother, artist Rex Whistler (1905–1944), who lived in The Close as a boy and was stationed at Codford training camp during the Second World War. He was killed in action prior to the D-Day Landings in France in 1944.

Walking Madonna (1981), the bronze sculpture by Dame Elisabeth Frink, is exhibited in Salisbury Cathedral Close. The figure is striding away from the church towards the town, 'walking with purposeful compassion as a member of the community of the Risen Christ, to bring love where love is absent'.

The Choice of Hercules (1636/37) by Nicholas Poussin at Stourhead, possibly once belonged to the architect François Blondel (1617–1686) and was bought by Henry Hoare II (1705).

Study of an Angel after Van Dyck (1750s) by Thomas Gainsborough, held in Wilton House, is based on the altarpiece *Saint Augustine in Ecstasy* (1628) in St Augustine's Church, Antwerp.

BOX TUNNEL

When Isambard Kingdom Brunel (1806–1859) was building the Great Western Railway, which ran between London and Bristol, one of the worst obstacles he faced was Box Hill. Its highest point was 400ft above the proposed level of the railway – the solution being a tunnel through a thick bed of oolite (Bath stone). It was the longest railway tunnel in existence, at almost 1.75 miles.

Work began on the tunnel in September 1836 and was finished by 30 June 1841 when the first train for public use made the journey from Bristol Temple Meads to Paddington in about four hours. Workers worked by candlelight and there were two teams working at each end with a combination of work by hand, with pick and shovel, and blasting. When they finally met in the middle, the roof lines coincided exactly and the sides were only fractionally out. Over 30 million bricks were used to complete the tunnel, made by local brickworks in Chippenham. The cost of driving the tunnel through Box Hill was, on average, £100 per yard. You do the maths!

The current titleholder for longest tunnel is the Seikan Tunnel in Japan which runs 33.49 miles, of which 14.5 miles run under the ocean.

CAEN HILL FLIGHT OF LOCKS

The title of 'longest flight of locks on a canal' nearly goes to John Rennie's 29 locks on the Kennet and Avon Canal. Its construction solved the problem of climbing 237ft up to Devizes, over a distance of 2.25 miles as part of the 87-mile route of the Kennet and Avon Canal. It opened in 1810 but fell into disrepair after the Second World War. After years of restoration work, the Queen opened the restored section on 8 August 1990. It received a Transport Trust Red Wheel plaque on 22 June 2011, marking its historical significance.

Tardebigge Flight on the Worcester & Birmingham Canal is the longest flight, with 30 locks raising the canal 220ft.

CROFTON PUMPING STATION

This Grade I listed building was built in 1807 to pump water to the summit of the Kennet and Avon Canal. The 42in Bore Boulton & Watt Engine built in 1812 is the oldest in the world still in working order.

HANDLE HOUSE

Teasels were used to finish cloth by raising the nap. They were mounted on wooden frames called handles and drawn over the dampened cloth. They were stored after use in buildings with ventilated walls. The Handle House in Stallard Street, Trowbridge, was probably built between 1843 and 1848 and is the only certain example of such a building in the West of England. With its exterior walls preserved, and a steel frame erected inside to stabilise it, the building has now been converted into offices.

RENAULT BUILDING

Also known as Spectrum, in Mead Way, Swindon, the Renault Building is Grade II listed and was designed by Norman Foster. It was built as Renault UK's parts distribution centre in 1983 at a cost of £8,266,400. The building has won four awards including the prestigious *Financial Times* 'Architecture at Work' Award (1984) and the Constructa Prize for Industrial Architecture in Europa (1986). It was used in the James Bond film, *A View to A Kill* (1985). Renault moved out in 2001 and it was temporarily used as an exhibition gallery for Swindon College and a Ford showroom. It is currently an indoor play centre run by Kidz About.

WILTON WINDMILL

Wilton is the only working windmill in Wessex. It was built in 1821 after the new Kennet and Avon Canal had been completed because the canal took the water that had formerly powered five local water mills. It was in operation for over 100 years but gradually fell into disrepair as milling methods changed with the advent of steam roller mills. It was restored by volunteers in 1976 and is currently owned by Wiltshire Council and managed by the Wilton Windmill Society. It still produces and sells stone-ground wholemeal flour. In 2003, scenes for Bollywood movie *Kuch Din Kuch Pal (Any Day, Any Time)*, starring Sudhanshu Panday and Bhumika Puri, were filmed there.

MILES OF BOOKS

The English Heritage Archive is housed in Swindon's former Great Western Railway drawing offices. It holds over 12 million items including photographs, drawings, reports and publications on England's archaeology, historic buildings and social and local history.

Housed on a former airfield acquired in 1979, the Science Museum at Wroughton is home to the Science Museum's big-object store, archive and library – one of the best science libraries in the world. It has 16 miles of shelving, displaying original editions including those by Einstein, Galileo, Newton and Darwin.

The Bodleian Libraries of the University of Oxford opened a new £26 million overflow Book Storage Facility (BSF) in Swindon in October 2010. The computerised and climate-controlled warehouse on the 23-acre site at South Marston can store 8 million low-usage books and maps on its 153 miles of shelving. Library staff use forklift trucks to retrieve books that are then transported to Oxford by road in a twice-daily service.

2

RECORD BREAKERS

FIRSTS

First King of England

Æthelstan (893/4–939) First King of all England. His grandfather was King Alfred the Great; his father King Edward the Elder. When his father died, his younger brother Elfweard succeeded to the throne and Æthelstan inherited the Kingdom of Merica. When his brother died he inherited everything, becoming King of Mercia and Wessex. He was crowned in Kingston upon Thames and reigned for fifteen years, having united all the English peoples under one rule. He did not marry and died aged forty-four in Gloucester. His tomb is in Malmesbury Abbey.

Beginning of the National Health Service

The Great Western Railway Locomotive Department Sick Fund was founded in 1843, the first health provision in New Swindon. It helped to pay workers during sickness and to meet funeral expenses through subscriptions deducted from wages. It was the model on which the NHS would be partly based 105 years later.

The First Man to Shoot Down a Zeppelin in the First World War

Highworth man Rex Warneford, a lieutenant in the Royal Naval Air Service, was on a bombing raid in Belgium on 6 and 7 June 1915, and attacked a German airship (Zeppelin), eventually dropping his bombs on it and bringing it down. He was awarded the Victoria Cross for this act. Highworth Warneford School is named after the local war hero.

First Female to be Charged with Speeding

The Hon. Mrs Victor Bruce (*née* Mildred Petre), aviatrix, motor racer and businesswoman who lived in Bradford on Avon (1950–1990), was fifteen when she was charged at Bow Street Magistrates' Court in 1911 for speeding at over 60mph on her brother's motorcycle.

First Arrest on the GWR Using Telegraphic Message

1 January 1845, Sgt William Williams of the Great Western Railway Police became the first person to make an arrest using the new technology. Alerted by a telegraph message sent from Slough, he arrested John Tawell who had murdered a girl at Slough, after he stepped off a train at Paddington.

First Test Cricket Century at Lord's

In 1848 Allan Gibson 'A.G.' Steel scored 148, the first ever Test Match century scored at Lord's Cricket Ground. He went to Marlborough College, where he started his cricketing career.

First Serving Soldier to Appear Topless in The Sun

Twenty-year-old Lance Corporal Roberta Winterton from Bridlington, Yorkshire, serving with 9 Supply Regiment at Hullavington Barracks, posed for *The Sun* published in February 2001.

Britain's Earliest Private Telephone

Soon after seeing Edison's published paper in 1877, describing his new invention of the telephone, Alfred Cunnington of Devizes made two telephones which connected his home at Southgate House with the family wine and spirit merchants in Wine Street.

The Only Communist Husband and Wife Urban District Councillors

Idris Rose, Trowbridge-born painter and decorator who lived in Stallard Street, was a Communist councillor on Trowbridge Urban District Council from 1961 until 1974, when the UDC was abolished. His wife Phyllis, also a communist, joined him on the council in 1969 and they formed the only husband and wife team of Communist urban district councillors in British history. The newspapers referred to them as 'Trowbridge's Red Roses' and 'Trowbridge's Red Menace'.

First Public School to go Co-Educational

Founded in 1843, Marlborough College was one of the first of the traditional boys' boarding schools to admit girls into the Sixth Form in 1968. It became fully co-educational in 1989. Catherine Middleton, Duchess of Cambridge, attended the sixth form, as did Princesses Eugenie and Beatrice.

First Steam Locomotive to Exceed 100mph

The Great Western Railway locomotive No 3440, City of Truro, designed by George Jackson Churchward, was built in 1903 at the GWR Works in Swindon. It was recorded on 9 May 1904 on its journey from Plymouth to Bristol, as going through the 100mph barrier, a record not broken again until the *Flying Scotsman* thirty years later.

Australia's First Postmaster

Calne-born Isaac Nichols (1770–1819) was convicted of stealing and sentenced to seven years' transportation at the Warminster Sessions in 1790. After his sentence expired, he was granted land in New South Wales and became a farmer, then superintendent of public works and an assistant naval officer. He was successful in preventing people fraudulently obtaining mail from incoming vessels and was appointed the colony's first Postmaster in 1809.

The First Genetically True Variety of English Malting Barley

Edwin Sloper 'Barley' Beaven (1857–1941) was a pioneer barley breeder and maltster who was born in Heytesbury and moved to Boreham Farm in Warminster. He produced the first genetically true variety of English malting barley called Plumage Archer. It was introduced to British farmers in 1905 and became the mainstay of UK malting barley production for the next fifty years.

The Earliest Poetic Celebration of the Alps Written in English

The Alps, by Trowbridge-born writer and painter George Keate, was published in 1763. An avalanche was described:

'The snowy Piles o'erwhelm him; frequent now,
At dead of Night, remote their sullen sound
Strikes on the startled ear … '

The Most Struck Bridge in the UK
Hullavington came second in 2005, with twenty-six strikes on the Kingway Railway Bridge, Malmesbury Road. First was Barrowby Road, Grantham, with thirty-two.

First Newspaper in Swindon and First Penny Paper in the Country
Swindon's first newspaper, the *Swindon Advertiser and Monthly Record*, appeared in 1854 as a monthly periodical, changing to a weekly paper called the *Swindon Advertiser and North Wilts Chronicle* after the removal of the Stamp Tax in 1855. William Morris (1826–1891), who was educated in the town and became its first historian, founded the 'Adver'. He was the sole writer, editor and printer of the paper, and went out selling it himself for a penny a copy. His great grandson is Desmond Morris, author of *The Naked Ape*.

First British Military Aeroplane Trials
In August 1912, Larkhill was the first military airfield in the UK to hold the first British military aeroplane trials. Samuel Franklin Cody, aka 'the Colonel', the showman and aeronautical designer from Iowa, took part in the Military Aeroplane Competition, winning the prize of £5,000 in his Cody Cathedral Biplane. The War Office purchased two of the planes which acquired code name 'British Army Aeroplane No 1'. Cody died in 1913 while testing a new design. He is buried in Aldershot Military Cemetery.

UK's First Philosophy Town
The first Thomas Hobbes Festival of Ideas took place in Malmesbury in 2008, as part of the bid to become the country's special Philosophy Town. In 2010, Professor Angie Hobbs was appointed one of the UK's first official town philosophers to what is now called Malmesbury Philosophy Festival.

First National Town Criers' Competition Winner
William Law, from Horsham, won the first ever national town criers' competition held in Devizes Market Place in February 1912. He received £5 and a new bell. John Knott, Devizes's town crier, came third but won first prize for the Handsomest Crier.

First School Production of Les Miserables

Dauntsey's School was the first school to stage the special school version of the musical *Les Miserables* in 2002, which they took to London for one night at the Prince of Wales Theatre. In 2012, Dauntsey's became the first school in Europe to stage the school edition of *Miss Saigon*.

First Blind Man Elected to Parliament

Salisbury-born Hanry Fawcett (1833–1884) was responsible for introducing the parcel post, the postal order and the first telegram.

Swindon's First Mural

Swindon-born artist Ken White was, for many years, personal artist to Richard Branson and became famous for his 'Scarlet Lady' emblem, designed for the launch of Virgin Atlantic in June 1984, which featured on all of the airline's aircraft. His early works included a series of murals in Swindon commissioned to record aspects of the town's history. His first one, painted in 1976, was a view of the Golden Lion Bridge on the end of a house in Fleming Way. It was part of a job creation scheme for Thamesdown Arts and has recently been restored by the artist.

First Funeral at Imber for Seventy Years

Florence 'Floss' Butcher (*née* Ayres), who died on 30 April 2012, aged eighty-one, was buried in her home village of Imber. The village had been evacuated in 1943 to house American troops preparing for the D-Day landings. Her funeral on 1 June 2012 at St Giles' Church was the first there for nearly seventy years.

SIZE MATTERS

The Biggest Meteorite to Land in the UK

A lump of stone which sat on the front step of the Lake House, Wilsford-cum-Lake, near Amesbury (owned by the Bailey family, 1928–1991) for more than eighty years, was identified in 2012 as the biggest meteorite found in the UK. Weighing 200lb and measuring 1.6ft long, it possibly came from a local barrow excavated by an archaeologist who lived at the house. The space rock may have landed on Earth 30,000 years ago, according to Professor Colin Pillinger from the Open University. It is currently on loan to Salisbury and South Wiltshire Museum.

Tallest Man in Britain
Frederick Kempster (1889–1918), aka 'The Great English Giant', was the fourth tallest man in history and possibly the tallest man ever in Britain. He joined Astley & Co.'s American Circus in Essex in 1911 and when he wasn't touring lived with his sister Ruth Rayner and her husband Jim in Essex, Bath and then Wiltshire at The Lodge (now Grange Lodge) Worton, the Barge Inn, Seend Cleeve, and the Red Lion Inn, Avebury. He was 7ft 9.5in in 1913, and reputedly 8ft 4in when measured by the Bath undertaker after his death. His 9ft coffin needed ten pallbearers. He wore size 22½ boots, his hand could span two octaves on a piano and a penny could be dropped through his finger ring.

The Tallest Building in Swindon
D.M.J. Tower (David Murray Jones Tower), better known as the Brunel Tower, stands 83 metres high, has 21 storeys and was completed in 1976. It was named after David Murray John, Clerk of Swindon Borough Council (1938–1974), in recognition of his work in Swindon's post-war regeneration.

Largest Cul-de-Sac in Europe
Monkton Park, Chippenham, lays claim to the title, as does Foley Road in Newent, Gloucestershire.

The Tallest Oak Tree in the UK
A 200-year-old English oak on the Stourhead estate was officially declared the tallest oak tree in August 2012. It measures 132.5ft.

The Most Spreading Tree in Britain
An Oriental Plane tree at Corsham Court covers an area the size of a football pitch, with a spread of over of 210ft. It has been identified as the most spreading tree in Britain, and possibly the largest in Europe. It was planted by Capability Brown in the 1760s during his work on landscaping the gardens and ground.

Largest Tortilla Chip in the UK
Chefs at Cepen Park Brewers Fayre, Chippenham, displayed the largest tortilla chip in the country to promote the opening of its Tex Mex menu in June 2012. The giant chip was made in their training and development kitchens in Swindon, where staff used 40kg of flour and 20 litres of water to create it. The end product weighed more than 50kg, measured 200 x 150cm and was equivalent to 10,000 normal-size tortilla chips.

Longest Continuous Dance

Teacher Ben Hammond, from Bradford on Avon, completed the world's first dance across Britain, from John O'Groats to Land's End (1,357 miles) on 27 July 2013. The charity challenge for LearnBurma had to be postponed in October 2012, after he was injured in a hit-and-run accident, 200 miles from the finish. He set a world record for the longest ever dance of 135 hours in central London, he was the first person to dance the London Marathon, and also danced 72 hours non-stop during the Glastonbury Festival 2011.

Largest Private Book Collection in Europe

Longleat House, one of the best examples of high Elizabethan architecture in Britain, and completed in 1580, has one of the largest private book collections in Europe, with over 40,000 books catalogued within its seven libraries.

Largest Single Collection of Roman Coins Found in One Container

In April 2010, Dave Crisp from Devizes, a member of Trowbridge & District Metal Detecting Club, discovered 52,503 Roman coins dating from AD 253 to AD 293, in a gigantic clay pot. Known as the Frome Hoard it contains a most unusual group of over 760 coins belonging to Britain's forgotten emperor, Marcus Aurelius Mausaeus Carausius, who declared himself Emperor of Britain from AD 286 to AD 293. Amongst them are five of the finest examples of silver Carausius denarii ever seen. The Frome Hoard, worth £320,250, is on display at The Museum of Somerset, Taunton.

BEST OF THE BUNCH

Top Six Film Locations
Castle Combe
Lacock Abbey and village
Salisbury
Stonehenge
Stourhead
Wilton House

One Rare Bible
A rare original 1611 King James Bible was discovered gathering dust on a shelf in St Laurence Church, Hilmarton near Calne, in March 2011 by a local resident researching the history of the church. Sadly, in 1857, the incumbent Revd Francis Fisher, although realising the book's importance, decided to make a beautiful carved oak cover for it and trimmed the pages of the Bible for a snug fit.

Best Bronze Age Archaeology Collection in Britain
The Wiltshire Heritage Museum in Devizes has the best Bronze Age archaeology collection in the country. Their Bush Barrow gold lozenge, which measures at 18 x 15cm and dates from 1900 BC, was discovered in 1808 by William Cunnington. It was featured in the top ten items in BBC *Wiltshire's History of the World in Ten Objects*. The replica currently on display will be replaced by the real deal in a new Neolithic gallery opening in 2013.

Finest Art Collection
Daniel Defoe, in his *A Tour Through The Whole Island Of Great Britain (1724–1726)*, extolled the virtues of Wilton House and gardens, but most of all the paintings. 'His Lordship (the Earl of Pembroke) is a great collector of fine paintings, so I know no nobleman's house in England so prepared, as if built on purpose to receive them; the largest, and the finest pieces.'

Loveliest Church in England
The Grade 1 listed St John the Baptist Church, Mildenhall (Minal), dating from the ninth century, was much praised by John Betjeman, and described by Simon Jenkins in his *England's Thousand Best Churches* (2000) as the 'loveliest of all the churches which remain untouched by the Victorians'.

Finest Example of Perpendicular Gothic Architecture
The Grade I listed thirteenth-century St Mary the Virgin Church, Steeple Ashton, is also included in Simon Jenkins' *England's Thousand Best Churches*, as an example of fine architecture.

One of the Best Collections of Lead Cloth Seals
Aside from the Museum of London, the Salisbury and South Wiltshire Museum houses the best collection of mediaeval lead cloth seals, as part of the city's Drainage Collection made up of artefacts found in the city's ancient drainage system channels in the nineteenth century. These seals were used to identify bales of cloths imported from this country and around the world.

Now in the British Museum
The fourteenth-century silver communion cup known as The Lacock Chalice, which belongs to St Cyriac's Church, Lacock, is displayed in the British Museum where it has been on loan since 1963.

One of the Gems of Anglo-Saxon Architecture
St Laurence's Church in Bradford on Avon, aka the Saxon Chapel, possibly dates from early eight century to mid-eleventh century. It is one of about seven complete Saxon churches in England and is regarded as 'outstanding'.

The Only Timber and Thatch Church in England
Said to be the only church constructed of timber and thatch, St Mary the Virgin and St Nicholas in Sandy Lane, Calne Without, was built in 1892 as a mission church at a cost of £170. Its features include a steep thatched roof and timbers constructed in an A form, with six pairs of trusses resting on brick sleeper walls. The walls of the church consist of two timber sections with sawdust rammed between.

Best Archive Services in the Country
The Wiltshire and Swindon History Centre, which opened in Chippenham in 2007, is the size of five small football pitches and has eight miles of archive material dating back 800 years. It was awarded a maximum four stars by The National Archives in 2011 and rated seventh out of a total of 124 services in England and Wales.

Best British Banger
'Malmesbury King' sausage, produced by Michael Thomas of Malmesbury, won the title Country Life's Britain's Best Sausage for 2010 – described as having 'the most pleasing, rustic, herby appearance and a satisfying, piquant taste'.

Strangest Art Collection

Alexander Thynn (formerly Thynne) 7th Marquess of Bath, who inherited the title and the Longleat estate in 1992, started painting in 1964. He recorded his life in murals and paintings, displayed on Bluebeard's Staircase in Longleat House. They included portraits of his many 'wifelets' (his term for mistresses) most with their heads severed. These and other artwork in the Paranoia and the Kama Sutra rooms were on show to the public until quite recently.

Most Historic Bus Route and Most Beautiful Bus Ride in the Country

The No. 49 Trans Wiltshire Express from Swindon to Trowbridge could claim this title – if there was one going! It begins where Brunel built the Great Western Railway, before travelling to the heart of Wiltshire's former wool trade, now the county town. Highlights of the journey are: Hackpen Hill White Horse; part of the Ridgeway; passing through the centre of Avebury Stone Circle; the view of Silbury Hill; going up Caen Hill, parallel to John Rennie's flight of 29 locks on the Kennet and Avon Canal; Wadworth's Brewery; and Devizes Market Place, one of the largest and most historic in the West.

OTHER TITLES AND RECORDS

Only Church Dedicated to St Cyriac in England

The fifteenth-century St Cyriac's Church in Lacock is the only church in England dedicated solely to the saint. St Cyriac, or Cyriacus, was a third-century Christian martyr who was killed in the persecution of the Roman Emperor Diocletian. He had been sent to relieve the suffering of slaves to the Emperor and was tortured with hot pitch being poured over him before he was beheaded on 8 August 304.

Longest-Serving Anchor Man

February 2012, Chris Vacher, presenter of BBC *Points West*, received a lifetime achievement award by the Royal Television Society for twenty-eight years of service for his outstanding contribution to television in the West of England region.

First Briton to Reach the South Pole, Solo and Unsupported

Swindon-born explorer David Hempleman-Adams, who lives in Box, set this record in 1996.

The Adventurer's Grand Slam, 1998

David Hempleman-Adams was the first man to reach Geographic and Magnetic North and South Poles and climb the seven highest peaks of the seven continents: Everest, Nepal; Mt Vinson, Antarctica; Aconcagua, Argentina; Carstenz Pyramid, Indonesia; Elbrus, Russia; and Kilimanjaro, Tanzania. He appeared on BBC's *Desert Island Discs* on 9 August 1998. His favourite disc was Stan Getz Mantua de Carnaval; his luxury, a saxophone, and his book, *Jonathan Livingstone Seagull* by Richard Bach.

Toy of the Year Award

In 1972 the title was awarded to Pelham Puppets of Marlborough.

World's Longest Running One-Man Radio Soap Opera

Acrebury (aka *The Wiltshire Archers*) entered *The Guinness Book of Records* in 1999. The series was set in the fictional village in the Fox Vale (based on Pewsey Vale) and ran from April 1974 to November 1985 on Swindon Hospital Radio, clocking up 600 episodes. It was resurrected on 4 April 1994 on BBC Wiltshire Sound (now BBC Wiltshire) where it ran for 1,558 episodes until August 2000. The show was created by Lyneham-born Gerry Hughes, now living near Devizes. He wrote, produced and acted all the parts (at least 150 characters), recording and editing the fifteen minute episodes at his home studio. For the 1,000th episode on 17 March 1998, there were commemorative mugs, framed prints and bars of *Acrebury* soap given away. The Paley Centre for Media (formerly the Museum of Television & Radio) holds archive episodes in New York and Los Angeles.

World Record Price for a Single Piece of Titanic *Memorabilia*
On 28 May 2011, Henry Aldridge & Son, in Devizes, sold the 32ft plan of RMS *Titanic*, which had been commissioned by the British Board of Trade for the enquiry into the sinking of the ship in 1912, for £220,000. In November 2012, another world record was set for a first-class menu from the first leg of the voyage from Southampton to Cork, realising £63,000.

Record Breaking Asian Art Auction
Salisbury auctioneers Woolley and Wallis's Asian Art sale on 25 May 2010 grossed £8.8 million, breaking the record for the highest grossing sale at a provincial auction house. An Imperial jade bell sold for £2.4 million, and a pair of jade elephants made £1.2 million. In April 2012 a pair of natural pearl earrings sold for £1.6 million – a record for any jewellery auction department outside London.

LAST BUT NOT LEAST

Last Tennis Ball Maker in Britain
J. Price Bath Ltd has been manufacturing tennis and squash balls since 1936. The family firm still has premises in Quarry Hill Works in Box, and is the only independent developer and manufacturer of tennis balls in Britain today.

The last Master Cooper in England
Alastair Simms, England's only working Master Cooper, worked at Wadworth & Co., Northgate Brewery, Devizes, from 1995 until 2013. He began his apprenticeship aged sixteen at Theakston's Brewery, North Yorkshire, qualifying as a Journeyman Cooper in 1983. In 1990 he took on an apprentice who qualified in 1994, thus making Alastair a Master Cooper. In 2010 Alastair was admitted into the Worshipful Company of Coopers.

Last Confession of Woman Hanged for Infanticide
Rebecca Smith of Bratton, aged forty-four, was found guilty of murdering her eleventh child, Richard, by arsenic poisoning on 12 June 1849. She was tried at the Assize Court, Devizes, and sentenced to death. While awaiting execution she confessed to the prison chaplain that she had murdered seven of her other children in the same manner. She was hanged outside Devizes prison on 23 August 1849.

Last Place You Want to Drive to

'The scariest junction in Britain' – the Magic Roundabout (originally called County Islands) consists of five mini roundabouts around a small central roundabout at the junctions of A4259 County Way, Queen's Drive, Fleming Way, B4289 Drove Road and Shrivenham Road. As a result of work by the Road Research Laboratory, under traffic engineer Frank Blackmore, the idea of the new Ring Junction was launched in 1972. His team first experimented with white painted lines and tyres, put into position to mark out the new junction. They were then able to watch the cars and lorries from a crane above to see what happened.

In 2005, Swindon's Magic Roundabout was voted the worst roundabout in the country by a UK insurance company. A survey of UK road users by the Highway Insurance Agency in December 2007 named it the 7th Most Feared Road Junction in the country, and in 2009, the fourth scariest junction in Britain in a poll by Britannia Rescue. The roundabout attracts visitors from around the world wanting to try the 'white-knuckle ride'. It is celebrated on various websites where you can buy 'I survived the Magic Roundabout' t-shirts, calendars, cards and sets of coasters depicting the iconic roundabout.

Last Wedding at Imber

The last wedding held at St Giles' Church in Imber was that of Bernie Wright and Phyllis Daniels on 27 November 1943. Residents of the village on Salisbury Plain were evacuated from their homes in December 1943 by the War Office to accommodate American troops preparing for the D-Day Landings – never to return.

Final Hooter for GWR Employees

Swindon's Great Western Railway Works' hooter, which summoned workers to the factory, replaced a bell in 1867; it sounded for the last time at 4.30 p.m. on 26 March 1986. Alfred Williams described it in *Life in a Railway Factory* (1915): 'The dreaded hooter bellows out, like the knell of doom to a great many. The sound travels to a great distance, echoing and re-echoing along the hills and up the valley seventeen or twenty miles away, if the wind is setting in that direction'. At 7.49 a.m. on Tuesday, 4 August 1914, ten blasts of the GWR Works' hooter signalled the beginning of the First World War. The twin domes of the historic hooter can still be seen on the rooftop close to the footpath to the Designer Outlet food hall.

3

MILITARY MATTERS

HERE AND NOW

The military is the biggest employer in Wiltshire. Wiltshire Council statistics show that the current (2012) military population in Wiltshire is 14,955 personnel, with 13,905 in the Army, 170 the Navy, and 880 the Air Force. The greatest numbers are stationed at the large army sites around Salisbury Plain Super Garrison (Tidworth, Perham Down and Ludgershall, Bulford Camp, Larkhill and Warminster, plus smaller stations at Upavon and Nertheravon). If you add dependents, the total military presence in Wiltshire is over 30,000, representing more than 6 per cent of the county's population.

ARMY TRAINING ON SALISBURY PLAIN

Now called the Defence Training Estate Salisbury Plain (DTESP) the area measures 25 miles by 10 miles and occupies about 1/9th of the county of Wiltshire. It covers an area just over 38,000 hectares (roughly the size of the Isle of Wight). Approximately 12,150 hectares is used for live firing and impact areas.

The War Office began purchasing land on Salisbury Plain in 1897 and completed its main acquisition programme by 1920; over the next thirty years the major garrisons were completed. The village of Imber was requisitioned by the War Office in 1943, and evacuated for use in training exercises for American forces for the D-Day landings. The residents (1931 census showed 152) never returned and the place has been used for military training ever since.

REHABILITATION

In August 2012, soldiers from The Rifles recuperating from their injuries in Afghanistan completed Operation Nightingale; part of Heritage Lottery funded Project Florence. This nine-month rehabilitation programme was set up by the Defence Infrastructure Organisation (DIO), English Heritage and Wessex Archaeology to excavate Barrow Clump (131ft barrow) on The Plain near Figheldean. They unearthed twenty–seven bodies, believed to be Anglo Saxon warriors, along with a variety of personal possessions such as gilt bronze brooches and amber beads.

WHAT A NERVE!

The War Department Experimental Ground at Porton Down on Salisbury Plain was the UK's first secret chemical warfare research establishment. It opened in March 1916, to provide a proper scientific basis for the British use of chemical weapons, in particular chlorine and phosgene and, later, mustard gas. The place had eight name changes over the years including Royal Engineers Experimental Station, Chemical Warfare Experimental Station, Chemical Defence Experimental Establishment, and the Chemical and Biological Defence Establishment. It is now called the Defence Science and Technology Laboratory (Dstl), Porton Down; its purpose is 'to maximise the impact of science and technology for the defence and security of the UK'.

Between 1920 and the end of the Second World War, the main emphasis was on researching mustard gas and its effects, and then on biological warfare. In the 1970s and 1980s its preoccupation was with defence against the nerve agents capable of exerting effects through the skin, the eyes and respiratory tract. From the first Gulf War onwards, it has been involved in chemical warfare research and technical support for the United Nations Special Commission set up to oversee the destruction of Weapons of Mass Destruction in Iraq.

In the 1950s, to test the effectiveness of nerve agents such as Sarin, servicemen were offered about £2 and a pass for three days extra leave if they volunteered to take part in tests, many believing it was part of a programme to find a cure for the common cold.

A verdict of unlawful killing on the death of twenty-year-old Leading Aircraftman Ronald Maddison was returned on 15 November 2004, the sixty-fourth day of a new inquest held at Trowbridge. The RAF engineer died on 5 May 1953 during secret nerve gas tests, after having drops of the nerve agent Sarin dabbed on his arm at the Porton Down chemical warfare testing facility. Such tests took place between 1939 and 1989.

'The most carefully hidden secret was the Satan Bug – a strain of toxin so deadly that the release of one teaspoon could annihilate mankind' so read a blurb for Alastair Maclean's thriller, *The Satan Bug* (1962), which was set in Morden Research Centre and said to be based on Porton Down.

In May 2012, it was reported that DSTL staff were taking on new roles as Rare Insect Monitors on the Down's grassland and wooded areas (classified as a Site of Special Scientific Interest). They are running a network of nine traps for flies, moths and other insects in collaboration with the Natural History Museum in London.

CIVIL WAR ROUND-UP

The counties of Gloucestershire, Somerset and Wiltshire were of prime importance during the English Civil War (1642–1651) for the supply of food, uniforms and munitions.

Warminster was a place of considerable activity during the Civil War, predominantly as a Parliamentarian garrison, whilst Devizes was a Royalist stronghold. The Battle of Roundway Down, 13 July 1643, was the most important Royalist cavalry victory of the war. Sir Ralph Hopton's Royalist army defeated Sir William Waller's Parliamentary forces, which had over double the number of men and was expected to win easily. However, caught in the middle of two Royalist forces many Parliamentarian soldiers just turned and fled. Six hundred lives were lost, mostly Parliamentarians, and 800-1,000 captured. This led to further victories by the Royalists in the Southwest.

During the Civil War and Commonwealth period (1649–1660), the Bishop, Dean and Chapter of Salisbury Cathedral were expelled and the cloisters and Chapter House were used to house Dutch prisoners of war.

In the churchyard of St Michael the Archangel, Mere, stands the stump of a medieval cross, destroyed in 1643 by Cromwell's soldiers in addition to fining two Mere men for taking the King's side.

They also imprisoned the vicar, Dr Thomas Chafyn, in 1645. He was badly treated and died from his injuries. The cross was later restored from fragments that had been used as boundary markers.

During the storming of Wardour Castle in 1644, a Royalist musketeer named Hilsdean was mortally wounded. As he lay dying, he suddenly realised to his horror that he had been shot by his own brother, who was a member of the Parliamentarian garrison.

Bromham House, the home of the Bayntun family, was deliberately destroyed by fire by Royalist troops from the Devizes Garrison, on 5 May 1645.

In 1646, Roundhead soldiers were billeted at The Scribbling Horse (now The Lamb) in Devizes, paying 10s for their board and lodgings.

During the Civil War, Malmesbury changed hands five times, with two direct assaults on the town itself. A reminder of these bloody times can be seen in the west end of the abbey where the south-facing wall to the side of the main porch is riddled with bullet holes, indicating where prisoners of war were executed.

EIGHT RESTORED FOVANT BADGE REGIMENTS

The restored regimental badges carved into the chalk downs above the village of Fovant by the soldiers of regiments stationed in the area during or soon after the First World War, can be viewed on the hillside of Fovant from the A303 Salisbury to Shaftesbury Road. They are:

Royal Wiltshire Yeomanry
6th Battalion, The City of London Regiment
Australian Imperial Force Badge
Royal Corps of Signals
The Wiltshire Regiment
London Rifle Brigade
The Post Office Rifles
The Devonshire Regiment

THE WILTSHIRE REGIMENT

The Wiltshire Regiment (Duke of Edinburgh's) was an infantry regiment formed in 1881 by the amalgamation of the 62nd (Wiltshire) Regiment of Foot (1756–1881) and the 99th Duke of Edinburgh's (Lanarkshire) Regiment of Foot (1824–1881); the 62nd Foot becoming the 1st Battalion, and the 99th becoming the 2nd Battalion. The regiment served in both world wars.

In the reduction of the Army after the Second World War, the Wiltshire Regiment was amalgamated with the Royal Berkshire Regiment in 1959, to form the Duke of Edinburgh's Royal Regiment (Berkshire and Wiltshire). There were further mergers in 1994, with the Gloucestershire Regiment, to form the Royal Gloucestershire, Berkshire and Wiltshire Regiment, and in 2006 with the Devonshire and Dorset Regiment to form the Royal Gloucestershire, Berkshire and Wiltshire Regiment Light Infantry. The most recent merger was in 2007 with the Royal Green Jackets and the Light Infantry to form the Rifles.

Four Regimental Nicknames
All Wiltshire battalions were known as the 'Moonrakers', a popular nickname for Wiltshire people after the local smugglers' legend (*see* Law & Order).

The 62nd (1st Battalion) were known as the 'Springers' based on their reputation for alertness and speed displayed in the American War of Independence in 1755, and also from the command to the light infantry to 'spring up' when advancing to attack.

The 99th (2nd Battalion) were known as the 'Queen's Pets', as they were favourites of Queen Victoria when guarding the Royal Pavilion in Aldershot in 1858. The expression 'dressed up to the nines' is said to come from their high standard of dress.

The 7th Battalion were known as the 'Shiny Seventh', the nickname coming from their reputation for high standards of dress and discipline instilled by Colonel Walter Rocke, who formed a new battalion in Marlborough of 'enthusiastic' volunteers (those recently retired and recalled).

Headquarters
Le Marchant Barracks, London Road, Devizes, was completed in 1878 at a cost of £46,000. It was named after Sir John Gaspard Le Marchant who commanded the 99th Regiment of Foot in 1839, later becoming part of

the Wiltshire Regiment in 1881, and was the regimental headquarters until 1959. Le Marchant Camp 23, a hutted transit camp about a mile from the barracks, housed up to 7,500 German and Italian prisoners of war in November 1944, many captured after the D-Day landings in the summer.

Regimental Music

One old Wiltshire song was adopted as a marching song by the 4th Battalion, TA 1st Volunteers Battalion of the Wiltshire (Duke of Edinburgh's Royal) Regiment and became the Wiltshire's unofficial anthem.

The Vly be on the Turmut

Twere on a jolly zummer's day, the twenty-fust o' May,
John Scroggins took his turmut-hoe, wi' thic he trudged away:
Now zome volks they likes haymakin', and zome they vancies mowin'–
But of all the jobs as I likes best, gi'e I the turmut-hoein'.

Chorus:
The vly, the vly,
The vly be on the turmut –
'Tis all me eye
Fer I to try
To keep vly off the turmut.

The fust place as I went to work, it were wi' Varmer Gower:
Who vowed and swore as how I were a fust-rate turmut-hoer;
The second place I went to work, they paid I by the job –
But if I'd knowed a little 'afore, I'd sooner a' bin in quod.

Chorus

The last place as I went to work, they sent fer I a-mowin',
I sent word back, I'd sooner take the zack, than gi'e up turmut-hoein'!
Now all you jolly varmer chaps wot bides at home so warm –
I'll now conclude my ditty wi' a-wishin' you no harm.

Chorus

MP's X Factor

When John Glen was elected MP for Salisbury in 2010, taking over from Robert Key (1983–2010), he continued the 300-year-old tradition of the newly elected candidate's appearance on the balcony of the White Hart Hotel to sing 'The Vly be on the Turmut'.

Smarten Up

From the 1772 Militia Orders & Instructions for the Wiltshire Battalions of Militia, Salisbury, 27 Oct 1759: 'Lord Bruce, having observed that the men appear in the streets with their hair untied, coats unhooked, stockings ungartered, hats slouched, handkerchiefs round their necks, and in all respects, in a very slovenly manner, orders that each company be divided into 4 squads with a sergeant and corporal to each squad who are to be answerable for the good appearance of the men in their squads.'

Trench Orders

From 1916 Trench Orders for the 2nd Battalion Duke of Edinburgh's Wiltshire Regiment: 'A Regiment should guard its trenches as closely as it guards its honour and its good name, and rather than surrender a foot to the enemy every officer, non-commissioned officer or private must be prepared to die in them. The word "retire" is never to be heard in a trench.'

SHELL SHOCKED

General Henry Shrapnel (1761–1842), army officer and inventor of the long-range artillery shell named after him, was born at Midway Manor House, Bradford on Avon. In 1785 he started work on developing his artillery shell containing lead or iron shot and using a delayed fuse. This enabled shells to be carried intact into enemy lines where they detonated, with devastating consequences. This shell was adopted by the British Army in 1803 and was praised by the Duke of Wellington for its effectiveness at the Battle of Waterloo. Shrapnel was buried in the family vault at Holy Trinity Church in Bradford on Avon, where there is also a brass memorial plaque. Shells were still being manufactured to his original design until the end of the First World War.

WAR WORK

Uniform Output

During the First World War, cloth production in Trowbridge changed to producing material for military uniforms. Messrs John and Thomas Clark Ltd, of Studley Mills, made large quantities of officers' and men's khaki, whipcord, serges, British warms, silver grey flannels, and Flying Corps clothing. Messrs Kemp & Hewitt Ltd, of Innox and Silver Street Mills, made khaki clothes for British, Belgian and American officers' uniforms, and blue-grey for the French officers' uniforms.

Nimble fingers

At Messrs G.N. Haden & Sons Engineers in Trowbridge such was the quality of the war work undertaken by women workers employed from July 1915 making high explosive shells, that no defective shell was returned by the Government during the thirteen months prior to the Armistice, which terminated the contract.

No smoking

Not long after the new No. 5 Wills Tobacco factory was opened in 1915 in Colbourne Street, Swindon (now a Tesco superstore), the Ministry of Munitions took over control (until 1919) and facilities were used for storing live shells. At one time there were over 3 million shells on the site.

In at the Deep End

Both pools were drained and boarded over at Milton Road Swimming Baths, Swindon, during the First World War and used by the Red Cross as hospital wards for wounded troops.

Your Country Needs You

Leonrad Raven-Hill (1867–1942) *Punch* cartoonist and illustator of Kipling's *Stalky & Co.*, lived at Battle House, Bromham (1896–1912). During the First World War he produced propaganda posters encouraging men to join the armed forces.

Protection

Twenty million gas masks were produced by Avon Rubber Co., in Melksham, during the Second World War.

From Carpets to Kitbags

From 1939–1945, the Wilton Carpet factory ceased production and took on war work, including washing army blankets and manufacturing camouflage, kitbags and tarpaulins.

Keeping the Ice Off

In 1941, Linolite, specialising in strip lighting for shelves and shaving lamps, moved from London to the Old Brewery site in Malmesbury to escape air raids. During the war, production was diverted to making hose-clips for bomber aircraft de-icing systems. They made 7.5 million of them but reverted back to making electric lights after the war. The factory moved to Tetbury Hill in 1985 but closed in 1993.

Spitfires

The original Spitfire manufacture took place in Southampton, but this well-known location made it vulnerable to enemy attack. The prototype (K5054) first flew on 5 March 1936. Most of the Spitfire production was moved to five areas, Trowbridge, Salisbury, Reading, Newbury and Swindon South Marston (now Honda).

During the war, the mark V, IX, XII and XIV Spitfires were built here, including, from 1944, the Griffon-powered version, as well as parts for the Supermarine 371. At least eight of the Spitfires built in Trowbridge still survive, four of which were found in India in the 1970s. One of these still appears in flying displays today. Named after the engines, Spitfire Park and Merlin Park are two retail parks built on the former factory sites.

Hangars at RAF Keevil airfield were used as a final assembly point before testing and dispersal.

THREE UNDERGROUND STORIES

In June 1941, part of the Royal Enfield Company moved from Redditch, Worcestershire, to the old Westwood Quarry near Bradford on Avon. The company changed to the manufacture of Type 3 Predictor sights for anti-aircraft guns and control equipment for Bofors guns. At the end of the war, the company continued to make motorcycles, initially from stocks of spare parts. The 250cc Crusader, Meteor and Meteor Minor models were made at Greenland Mills, Bradford on Avon, until 1963; the Interceptor made at the former Wilkins brewery in Newtown; and the Constellation at Westwood until 1970.

From February 1942, another part of Westwood Quarry was used for the safe storage of art, artefacts, printed books, manuscripts, prints and drawings evacuated from places such as the British Museum, the Victoria and Albert Museum, and the Bodleian Library. Visiting at that time, there would have been Greek statues, medieval tapestries, a Rubens ceiling from a Whitehall banqueting hall and the Wright Brothers' airplane 'Flyer' or 'Kitty Hawk', which had been on loan from the Science Museum since the beginning of the war.

A nuclear bunker was built at the height of the Cold War in the basement of the new Devizes Library, which opened on 27 November 1968. It was designed to house councillors and officers of the former Devizes Rural District Council.

CHEERS!

Ushers Brewery in Trowbridge had its own fire engine and crew which, during the Second World War, formed a crew within the National Fire Service and served in Bath during the blitz of the city.

In March 1993, Ushers Brewery airlifted a consignment of ales to the former Yugoslavia to boost the spirits of the 360 men serving for the Ordinance Battalion, Cheshire Regiment, in Split and to the United Nations workers in Sarajevo.

In 2010, Ramsbury Brewery in Aldbourne produced a special beer called '506' as a tribute to the American 506th Parachute Infantry Regiment of the 101st Airborne Division. During 1943, in preparation for D-Day, the Regiment was accommodated in Ramsbury, Chilton

Foliat and Froxfield. The beer label shows the regiment's spade emblem and their motto 'Currahee', Cherokee for 'stand alone'.

LEST WE FORGET

Nineteen-year-old Sergeant Hubert Arthur Whatley of the 53rd Squadron, Royal Flying Corps, was shot down by 'Red' Baron von Richthofen on 2 July 1917. His death is recorded on the war memorial at St John the Baptist Church in Pewsey.

The War Grave Cemetery at Codford St Mary is the second largest in the UK. There is one First World War grave of a Welsh guardsman, and ninety-seven ANZAC troops (sixty-six from New Zealand and thirty-one for Australia) most of whom died from sickness, presumably the Spanish flu.

Warminster's War Memorial, unveiled 29 May 1921, is a 21ft-high Iona-type cross made of Box-ground Bath stone, incorporating interwoven rope work and Egyptian art. The designer was local stonemason Egerton Strong whose ancestors worked with Sir Christopher Wren on rebuilding St Paul's Cathedral after the Great Fire of London. The monument was re-dedicated on 6 November 1949 when the names of townsmen lost during the Second World War were added.

In July 1947, at the time of his engagement to Princess Elizabeth, Prince Philip was instructing cadets at the petty officer training school HMS *Royal Arthur* in Corsham. His first public engagement on 1 November 1947 was opening the World War Two Garden of Remembrance in Stokes Road, Corsham.

The war memorial in Wootton Bassett (now Royal Wootton Bassett) was unveiled in October 2004. Calne artist Vivian ap Rhys Price made the bronze sculpture of a globe held by two pairs of hands mounted on a stone pedestal. The design by fifteen-year-old Lance Cpl Alan Wilson of the Wootton Bassett Army Cadets was decided by public vote. The globe shows past and present places of conflict where the British have fought.

The Rifles (Berkshire and Wiltshire) Museum in Salisbury has several artefacts relating to the Holocaust. One is a door-locking bolt mechanism and spring from the crematorium at Bergen-Belsen Concentration Camp, where more than 50,000 prisoners died. The 4th Battalion Wiltshire Regiment was one of the first to liberate the camp in April 1945, setting up a base camp there to assist with relocating the prisoners, as well as clearing and cleaning the camp.

Captain Lord John Arundell, of the Wiltshire Regiment and 16th Baron of Wardour, was wounded and taken prisoner at Dunkirk in 1940. He was held in Colditz Castle before being repatriated to Britain in 1944, where he died of TB soon after. Without an heir, on his death, his title dating back to 1605 became extinct.

Guy Gibson (1918–1944), one of the RAF's youngest Wing Commanders, who led 617 Squadron in the Dam Busters raid in May 1943, was trained at the Service Flying Training School at RAF Yatesbury (1936/37). He was killed in September 1944 while leading a raid of 230 Mosquitoes and Lancasters over Holland, in what was later revealed as a result of 'friendly' fire when his Lancaster was mistaken for a German plane.

FAREWELL, RAF LYNEHAM

Home of the UK's military air transport operations
Support-Save-Supply (1943–2012)
Home of the Hercules Tactical Transport Aircraft (1967– 2011)

James Gray, MP for North Wiltshire: 'We in Wiltshire will say a sad farewell to the RAF. The nearby Yatesbury base still has the First World War Officers' mess and hangars of the RAF, which was founded there roughly 100 years ago. Ever since then the RAF has had a home in Wiltshire. Sadly, when it leaves Lyneham later this year a long and distinguished link with the RAF will end.'

Hansard, 26 January 2011

Herculean tasks

The Lockheed C-130 Hercules, aka Fat Albert (possibly after American comedian Bill Cosby's creation Fat Albert and the Cosby Kids in 1972), arrived at RAF Lyneham on 1 August 1967. The four-engine tactical support aircraft is capable of carrying up to 92 ground troops, 64 paratroops, 74 stretcher cases, or a variety of vehicles and freight up to 20 tons in weight over distances of up to 4,600 miles at speeds in excess of 370 knots. More than 2,200 C-130s have been built during this, the longest production run of a particular aircraft in history. It is an extremely versatile aircraft and is used by more than 60 of the world's air forces.

Hostages' Homecoming

Journalist John McCarthy, who had been held hostage in the Lebanon from April 1986 to August 1991, returned and landed at RAF Lyneham on 8 August 1991.

Former Second World War Spitfire pilot, Jackie Mann, who was living in Lebanon and running a riding school with his wife, had been held hostage in the country from May 1989 to September 1991, returned and landed at RAF Lyneham on 26 September 1991.

Church of England envoy Terry Waite, who had been held hostage in the Lebanon for January 1987 to November 1991, returned and landed at RAF Lyneham on 19 November 1991.

Three Unusual Cargoes

2,000 coat hangers, along with 6,000 pairs of ladies underwear (all the same size but available in three different colours), were transported to Harare in newly independent Zimbwabe (formerly Rhodesia) in 1980, on a 5,503-mile journey.

In 1980, Hereford and Worcester Fire Brigade donated an eleven-year-old red fire engine (still serviceable) to the Harare Fire Brigade in Zimbabwe, which went out by Hercules from Lyneham.

To celebrate the 200th anniversary of American Independence in 1979, as part of Exercise Cold Link, LXX Squadron took part in a squadron exchange with the Green Weasels Squadron at USAF Base Dyess, Texas. The Lyneham crew took a gift of a red Victorian post box, acquired from Bath Post Office and restored. The post box is still in use on the base, a little bit of England 'deep in the heart of Texas'.

A PEACEFUL CONCLUSION

Blakehill Farm Airfield, near Cricklade, was one of the most important airfields of the Second World War and became home to two RAF squadrons that played key roles in the D-Day landings of 5 June 1944. The area has now become the largest neutral grassland restoration project in Europe, thanks to the work of Wiltshire Wildlife Trust. The sound of Dakotas has long gone, and Skylarks and Curlews now fill the air. Military activity was replaced by hares and fallow deer enjoying the freedom of fields, and hedgerows filled with Grizzled Skipper butterflies.

4

LAW & ORDER

MOONRAKER LEGEND

Wiltshire smugglers in the late eighteenth century, who were trying to evade excise men on their trail from Bristol, hid their casks of brandy in a village pond, said to be near Devizes (possibly the Crammer). When they returned the next evening to retrieve them, a policeman caught them trying to rake the casks out of the pond. When asked what they were doing, they pointed at the moon's reflection in the water and said that they were trying to get 'that gurt big cheese out'. The policeman, assuming they were simpletons, went off laughing at the men's stupidity, leaving them free to retrieve their casks.

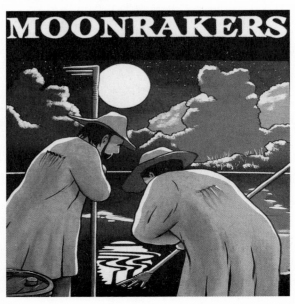

DEADLY RE-ENACTMENT

The first Hang Day Fayre was held at the Bell Inn, Purton Stoke, on 29 September 2007. It included a re-enactment of the events surrounding the murder of Stephen Rodway, a salt and coal merchant from Cricklade, by bare-knuckle fighter Robert Watkins from Wootton Bassett, on 7 May 1819. At the Salisbury Assizes, Watkins was found guilty of murdering Rodway who was shot in an attempted robbery at Moor Stones (now called Watkin's Corner). The body was taken to the Bell Inn for the autopsy. Between 10,000 and 15,000 people came to Purton Stoke to see Watkins hanged on 30 July 1819, and 200 special constables were sworn in for the occasion, in case of trouble. Later, Watkins's father confessed to the crime.

CRIME & PUNISHMENTS

Salisbury Martyrs 1556
John Foxe's *Acts and Monuments*, aka the *Book of Martyrs* (1563), recorded the execution of three Wiltshire 'heretics' (against the newly reinstated Catholic faith by Mary Tudor) who had disrupted a church service at Keevil Church and incited parishioners to abandon a procession. John Spicer, freemason, William Coberley, tailor, and John Maundrel, husbandman, were taken from Fisherton Gaol to Bemerton Field where they were chained to stakes and burned to death on 24 March 1556.

Swearing and Other Crimes
Between 1697 and 1820, 13 per cent of crimes in Wiltshire were for swearing.

1758   John Clutterbuck, Melksham fined 3s for swearing.
1763   Harrold Hester, spinner, Bulkington, fined 10s for cursing.

Apart from swearing, petty thefts of food and fuel, acts of poaching and killing game, traffic offences, vagrancy, and the mis-selling of goods kept Wiltshire magistrates busy.

1744   Joseph Marchmentt, Pewsey, 3 days gaol for selling beer and ale without licence.
1756   Sarah Pierce, Burbage, fined 7s 6d and whipt for stealing hedge wood.
1780   William Cowley, Ramsbury, fined 6s for selling bread under weight.

1784	Stephen Reynolds, turnpike toll gatherer, Warminster, fined £10 for not reporting refusal to pay toll.
1798	Robert Knight, driver, Maiden Bradley, fined 10s for allowing wagon drawn by too many horses.
1797	Joseph Mayall, travelling hawker, Warminster, fined £10 for handbills without 'licensed hawker'.
1804	Richard Homes, cooper, Wootton Bassett, fined £10/5 12s for wearing hat not stamped. (The 1803 Act was introduced to raise duty on hats. Sellers needed licences which cost £1 in town, and 5s in other areas. Fines were high at £50. The Act was repealed in 1811.) Presumably, Richard was wearing a hat that had fallen off the back of a cart!
1806	John Johnson, maltster, Bishopstone, fined £103 for sprinkled water on barley for malt.
1809	George Webber, dyer, Trowbridge, fined for throwing firework in street.
1810	Hannah Jones, Bradford, fined £1 for stealing turnips.
1816	Edward Edge, Kennet & Avon Canal, fined £2 for not shutting sluices on lock after boat.

Horse Stealing, 1801

Gypsy Joshua Scamp was hanged for horse stealing, protesting his innocence to the end. Unusually, he was buried in the churchyard of St Mary's Church in Odstock where the parish register records: '4 April 1801: Joshua Scamp, a gypsy, hanged supposed wrongfully.' It is said that he was protecting his son-in-law, who later confessed to the crime.

Passing Forged Banknotes, 1805

William Cox, thirty-four-year-old native of Atworth, had been engaged some time in passing bad notes, which he accomplished by attending fairs and markets, as a horse dealer. He sold a pony at Tinhead, for which £10 note was given him in payment. He then passed a £5 forged note in exchange. He was executed for his crimes.

Execution Draws Record Crowd, 1824

The *Devizes Gazette* reported the execution of Edward Amor and John Goodman at Devizes for robbery and assault on 24 December 1823. 'On Tuesday last (in April) these two unfortunate men, convicted of robbing and brutally assaulting Mr Thomas Alexander, of All Cannings, were executed in front of the Penitentiary, near this town. The number of people assembled to witness the awful scene amounted to between 20 to 30,000; indeed, it appeared as if the whole county had poured forth its contents. Long before the appointed hour, the large yard before the prison, and the adjoining road, for a long space, were entirely filled. Being the first execution that has taken place in this neighbourhood, its occurring on Easter Tuesday, and Devizes Green Fair being held on that day, all tended to increase the number of spectators.'

Selling a Wife, 1833

Isaac Spencer, who believed that selling a wife publicly in the market place with a halter round her neck would have full force of a divorce legally obtained, took his wife (equally willing to try a change of circumstances) to the public market at Melksham and there disposed of her for 2s 6d to a man named William Watts. Both were committed to prison for the offence, but Watts was acquitted.

HIGHWAY ROBBERY

Pressing Engagement, 1743

Charles Taylor who plied his 'trade' in the Cherhill Downs area was sentenced to *peine forte et dure* (pressing to death by weights) at Salisbury Assizes in July 1743 for his refusal to plead to two robberies of £50 and £20. This was then reduced to the 'milder' form of twisting and screwing the thumbs with whipcord. The first knot of whipcord broke from the strain put upon it; the sight of the second knot brought to continue the torture did the trick. Taylor consented to plead and was later executed.

Femme Fatale, 1779

Mary Sandall (aka Mary Abrahams) who lived at Baverstock near Wilton used to dress as a man and carry a blunderbuss for her criminal activities. She liked to target women returning from selling their produce at local market. She was finally caught and sentenced to death for her attack on a Mrs Thring, later reduced to life imprisonment.

Kindly Gesture, 1783

Mr Reuben Sidney of Southampton was coming from Shaftesbury to Salisbury on Sunday morning 30 November 1783, when he was robbed near Fovant Hut by three footpads stealing eight guineas. On complaining to them of his lack of money to get home they returned him one guinea.

Stealing the Show

The Flying Highwayman, Thomas Boulter, was born in Poulshot about 1748 and was known for his good looks, good manners and tailored clothes. He is thought to have been behind the hold-up of a coach full of actors on their way from Bath to Salisbury. In spite of the theft of scenery and props the show went ahead. In one robbery, Boulter was partially blinded when shot in the face by a passenger defending himself. He was eventually caught with his partner, James Caldwell, and hanged in Winchester on 19 August 1778.

The Robber's Stone, Chilterne Down, 1839

This Monument is erected
to record the awful end of
BENJAMIN COLCLOUGH
a Highway Robber who fell
Dead, on this Spot, in
attempting to escape his
Pursuers after Robbing
Mr Dean of Imber, in the
Evening of Oct 21st 1839,
and was buried at Chitterne
without Funeral Rights.
The robbery of the wicked
shall destroy them.
Prov. 21. 7

His three companions in
Iniquity
THOMAS SAUNDERS
GEORGE WATERS &
RICHARD HARRIS.
were captured & sentenced
at the ensuing Quarter
Sessions at Devizes to
Transportation for the
Term of Fifteen Years.
Though hand join in
hand the wicked shall
not be unpunished
Prov. 11. 21

Farmer Dean, of Imber, was held up by four highwaymen on his way home from Devizes Market on 21 October 1839. Courageously,

he fended them off with his riding whip, calling out 'George! George!' – there was nobody called George. He was deceiving them into thinking he was not alone. After the robbers took off, he chased one of them for miles across the downs, the robber eventually dropping dead. Two stones were erected in memory of this event; the first stone marks this spot, the other where the robbers were caught and transported.

The Ghostly Drummer

There is a legend from the 1660s, that a drummer was arrested while begging in Tidworth and thrown into gaol at Salisbury. Because the drummer had no money to pay for food himself, or family or friends to bring him food, he starved to death. The sound of his drumbeat was heard in the house of the magistrate who sentenced him, so they say. Drummer Lane in Tidworth is a reminder of this local story.

Bloody Past

Morgan's Hill near Calne is supposed to be named after John Morgan, who robbed and murdered his uncle in 1720 and was hanged from the gallows on the hill before a large crowd. Now the place forms part of a Wiltshire Wildlife Trust nature reserve that has been helping to increase the population of butterflies with its wildflower seed-sowing scheme introduced in 2009.

The Wrath of the Almighty

On 25 January 1753, Potterne resident Ruth Pierce fell dead in Devizes Market Place in strange circumstances. She had agreed to buy a sack of wheat with three other women and when asked for her share of 4/3d declared that she had already paid it, twice adding that 'she wished she might drop down dead if she had not'. And so she did drop down dead, and a jury concluded that she had been struck down by 'the Visitation of the Great and Almighty God'. It is quite possible that she had paid and suffered a heart attack or stroke, which would not have been understood then. She is commemorated on the side of the Market Cross presented to the town by Henry Addington MP in 1814.

Centenarian Poacher

Anne Simons of Studley, near Calne, who died aged 113 in 1785, was still walking from Studley to Bowood a few months before her death. She was a well-known local poacher who often boasted of selling gentlemen the fish she had taken from their own ponds.

Wiltshire's First Serial Killer

Thomas Burry, who died in 1842, was landlord of The Shepherd and Dog on the Lydeway, near Urchfont, and was thought to have murdered solitary visitors to his hostelry. Some say that over a dozen bodies of his supposed victims were found in shallow graves behind the inn.

BLIND HOUSES

A blind house was a village gaol or lock-up, so called because it had no windows. Usually constructed of stone blocks, with heavy wooden doors, a domed roof and finial decoration on top, it was generally used for detaining drunks and troublemakers overnight. Most of the Wiltshire blind houses date from the eighteenth century.

Bradford on Avon. Originally built as a chapel for the nearby leper hospital at St Margaret's, continuing as a chapel for pilgrims, it is unique as it is part of the bridge over the river. John Aubrey wrote in his *Topographical Collections* (1659–1670): 'Here is a strong and handsome bridge in the middest of which is a little chapell as at Bathe, for Masse'. It eventually became the town lock-up.

Bromham. Built in 1809 at a cost of £16, this one is unusual as it is built into the churchyard wall of St Nicholas, made of wood and set on brick foundations.

Shrewton. Built around 1700 in Maddington Street, it was hit by a tank during the Second World War. It was moved brick by brick in the 1980s and rebuilt further back on the main road.

Steeple Ashton, aka the Guard House, was built in the centre of the village in 1773 and cost £19 18s.

Trowbridge. Built around 1758. An 1812 invoice from William Webb, Overseer of the Parish, showed that 1*s* 2*d* was spent on padlocks for the stocks, 4*s* 6*d* for a pair of hand bolts and 5*s* for straw for bedding for the prisoners.

There are also lock-ups in Box, Heytesbury, Hilperton and Lacock, and either side of the entrance to Malmesbury Abbey.

BOBBIES

Sir Robert Peel (1788–1850) twice Prime Minister (1834–1835 & 1841–1846) was MP for Chippenham from 1812 to 1817. While in office as the Home Secretary (1822–1827) he introduced many penal reforms and created the Metropolitan Police Force, thus giving his name to 'bobbies' or 'peelers', slang names for the police. He was also responsible for the introduction of the 1842 Mines Act which forbade the employment of women and children underground, and the 1844 Factory Act which limited working hours for children and women in factories.

THE OLDEST COUNTY FORCE
IN THE COUNTRY

The Force 'serves a population of 635,000 people across 1,346 square miles from Swindon's lively urban areas to the rolling countryside and iconic sites such as Stonehenge.'

Wiltshire Police, 2012

Wiltshire remains one of the top five forces in England which has the lowest number of crimes per 1,000 people (in 5th place), and the county is placed 6th in the country for offences of violence against the person per 1,000 of the population. (2011/12)

Wiltshire police force was founded in 1839 with the first Chief Constable, Commander Samuel Meredith, appointed on an annual salary of £400. A constable was paid 17s 6d a week, plus clothing.

Captain Robert Sterne RN became the second Chief Constable in 1870 and his administrative headquarters were at Northgate House in Devizes.

In 1871, a tour of inspection of police stations found that Malmesbury was the cleanest and Trowbridge the dirtiest.

Police hats were replaced by helmets in 1879.

In April 1892, the first police officer to die while on duty was Sergeant Enos Molden who was shot while attempting to arrest John Gurd for the murder of Harry Richards, the uncle of his fiancée. There is a memorial to Molden at Christ Church Warminster.

Due to conscription, the Wiltshire Constabulary became seriously undermanned, and by 1918 there were 92 vacancies out of a total force of 295.

A boot allowance of 1s a week was introduced in July 1918 for members of all ranks of the Wiltshire Constabulary.

A constable of the Wiltshire Constabulary was dismissed at Castle Combe for carrying on a business as a grocer and provision merchant and retailer of pigs' offal in High Street, Castle Combe, in 1919.

A constable of the Wiltshire Constabulary stationed at Ludgershall was severely reprimanded for playing cricket with civilians in July 1919. Playing cricket outside the force was strictly forbidden.

The first female police officer was forty-five-year-old former schoolmistress Miss Florence Mildred White, who was appointed to the Salisbury City Force in 1918. It wasn't until 1942 that the first female officers were recruited into the Wiltshire Constabulary.

First police patrol car, a five-seater Ford saloon costing £272, was introduced in 1920.

First patrol motorbikes were introduced in 1927.

First police dogs were introduced in Swindon, Salisbury and Trowbridge in 1951.

Elizabeth Neville was appointed Chief Constable of Wiltshire in 1997, the second woman in the country to be appointed to that post. She was awarded the Queen's Police Medal in 1996 and created a Dame in 2003, retiring in 2004.

In 2010 there were 1,180 officers, 140 support officers and 100 police staff serving the county of Wiltshire.

IN THE AIR

The Wiltshire Air Ambulance, or Wiltshire Police Helicopter, service began in 1990. It is currently a joint venture between Great Western Ambulance Service and Wiltshire Police, with 65 per cent funded by the Wiltshire Police and the other 35 per cent funded by the Wiltshire Air Ambulance Appeal (WAA) through fundraising. However, by 2015 it will have to fund all of the £2.5 million running costs itself, as the government is forming a National Police Air Service.

Four Flying Facts
The helicopter is a McDonnell Douglas 902 Explorer with two Pratt & Whitney engines (capable of flying on one engine if the other fails).

It has no tail rotor (NOTAR) making it quieter and easier to land.

It can go up to a speed of 180mph but usually cruises at 140mph with a range of 1.5 hours.

The crew can scramble in less than two minutes and can reach anywhere in the county within twelve minutes but in most cases it can do it in seven minutes.

A Day in the Life of the Air Ambulance
March 2012:
Horse rider injured, with suspected spinal and pelvic injuries, airlifted from Colerne to Bath in under five mins.
Soldier injured in landrover crash at Tidworth camp. Transported by road.
Patient with serious neurological symptoms airlifted to GWH for specialist care.
Elderly female collapsed unconscious in Marlborough treated by crew.

TWO MEMORIALS TO FALLEN OFFICERS

A plaque outside Trowbridge Police Station commemorates thirty-two-year-old PC123 Desmond Kellam who was killed on 3 October 1979, the third Wiltshire Police Officer to die while on duty. He had been investigating a burglary in Church Walk and died after an attack with a bill-hook administered by David James, who had just broken into WHSmiths. James was cleared of murder and sentenced to eight years for manslaughter.

A memorial window in St Leonard's Church, Semley, commemorates twenty-five-year-old WPC Yvonne Fletcher who was shot and killed while policing an anti-Gaddafi demonstration outside the Libyan Embassy in London on 17 April 1984. She was born in Semley in 1958 and served in the Metropolitan Police Force. An eleven-day siege followed the shooting, and eventually twenty embassy staff were allowed to leave the UK under diplomatic immunity laws. Investigators believe the bullet which killed Yvonne Fletcher was fired from inside the embassy by a sniper from a first-floor window. No one was brought to trial for the crime, although President Gaddafi accepted responsibility and paid compensation to her family in 1999. In 2012, a team from Scotland Yard was sent to Libya to re-investigate the murder.

DEFENDING HUMAN RIGHTS

Joel Joffe, Baron Joffe of Liddington, a human rights lawyer, lives in Liddington near Swindon. He was born in South Africa and defended Nelson Mandela in the famous Rivonia trial (1963–1964), named after the suburb of Johannesburg where sixteen leaders of the African National Congress had been arrested in July 1963 for acts of sabotage designed to 'ferment violent revolution'. Mandela, along with the others, received life sentences.

Ludovic Kennedy (1919–2009), writer and broadcaster, wrote several books highlighting miscarriages of justices. One case was George Davis, wrongly convicted of armed robbery and freed in 1976. Another was Timothy Evans who was hanged in 1950 for the murder of his wife and baby daughter. He was given a posthumous royal pardon in 1966, although attempts to quash his conviction failed. Kennedy's exposure of the case was said to have played a part in turning public opinion and Parliament against the death penalty. He married dancer and actress Moira Shearer of *The Red Shoes* fame and moved to Avebury in the 1980s where they lived for over eighteen years. He was knighted in 1994.

Weapons Amnesty, October 1961
During the first two months of a weapons amnesty for the surrender of firearms, Chippenham Police Station received 58 revolvers, 13 rifles, 1 machine gun, 2,728 rounds of ammunition, 3 grenades, and 1 other firearm, as well as a rifle grenade from the First World War and a German mortar bomb.

5

WORKING LIFE

SUCCESS STORIES

Cardinal Thomas Wolsey (1471–1530), Archbishop of York and Lord Chancellor of England, was ordained at St Peter's Church, Marlborough, on 10 March 1498. He became chancellor to Henry VIII (1514–1529) and in 1515 Pope Leo X made him a cardinal. He was held partly responsible for failing to persuade the Pope to agree to Henry's divorce and was arrested for treason in 1530 but died before his trial.

Wiltshire was once famed for its clay pipes and those made by the Gauntlet family of Amesbury in particular were well respected by smokers in the seventeenth century. In 1622, historian Thomas Fuller described them as 'the best for shape and colour'. Made from clay dug on the downs of Chitterne St Mary, they were stamped with their own mark: the outline of a right-hand gauntlet.

Clockmaker Edward Cockey of Warminster (1669–1768) was best known for a series of great astronomical clocks which stood 10ft tall. One was made for Thomas Thynne, Viscount Weymouth at Longleat, and described in a 1719 inventory: 'Great Parlour. A fine clock in a Japan'd case showing ye change of ye moon, rising and setting of ye sun and its course thro ye zodiac.' Another one, a signed example housed in a later mahogany case, made in about 1760, is part of the Ilbert Collection at the British Museum. A third one is thought to have been presented to Queen Anne.

Reputedly one of the wealthiest commoners in Britain, Sir Samuel Fluyder (1704–1768), cloth merchant and MP for Chippenham (1754–1768), Director of the Bank of England and Lord Mayor of London was worth £900,000 (equivalent to over £57 million in 2005) on his death in 1768.

Mr W. Boxall wrote a letter entitled 'Efficacy of the Purton Spa Water in Heptacic Colic' to the *Medical Times and Gazette* (1862) giving an account of his successful treatment of a forty-six-year-old woman from New Swindon: 'Her bilious ailments now no longer continue to distress her, and she is again able to discharge the duties of her household with comparative ease.'

Car tyres produced by Avon India Rubber Co. Ltd, Melksham, were advertised for the first time in *Autocar* magazine in 1906.

HM Queen Mary visited Ashton and Court Mills, Trowbridge, on 17 September 1943 and was presented with a length of cloth woven in Clan Urquhart tartan.

Architect Sir Norman Foster won the *Financial Times* 'Architecture at Work' Award in 1967 for his design of the Reliance Controls Electronics Factory, Greenbridge, Swindon. The building was demolished in 1991 to make way for a PC World.

Chippenham Civic Society unveiled a blue plaque in September 2010 at Ivy Lane School to commemorate Robin Tanner, 'Renowned Etcher and Educationalist', who taught at the school from 1929 to 1935. He lived with his wife, Heather, a writer and peace campaigner, at Chapel Field in Kington Langley from 1932 until his death in 1988. His etching plates are held in the Ashmolean Museum.

The Badminton Game by artist David Inshaw, painted not long after moving to Devizes in 1971, was acquired by the Tate Gallery in the 1980s. As a public work of art, it was chosen to hang in 10 Downing Street during John Major's term of office (1990–1997).

If you've ever walked across Sydney Harbour Bridge, you will undoubtedly have had to strap yourself into one of the ManSafe safety fall arrest systems harnesses made by Latchways of Devizes (founded in 1974). Other tourist spots where you'll find their fall protection equipment are Disneyworld, the London Eye and Spain's Port Aventura.

LOST JOBS & DYING ARTS

Bird & Animal Preservers
Henry Hussey, Easterton, 1920

Cooper
Jacob White, Pippit St, Bradford on Avon, 1830

Dewpond Digger
Jacob Smith, Market Lavington, 1891

Gramophone Dealer
Mercer Bros, Milton, Pewsey, 1907

Hockey Stick Maker
Crosby & Jennings, High Street,
Marlborough, 1920

Ice Dealer
Edwin Karley, 2 Brittox, Devizes, 1907

Inspector of Windows (Windows were taxed from 1696 to 1851; also referred to as 'Daylight Robbery' as people blocked up windows to avoid payment.)
William Kendall, Devizes, 1793

Lace Menders
Boden & Co. Ltd, Castle Street, Mere, 1920

Legging and Gaiter Manufacturer
R. Ockwell, High Street, Cricklade, 1907

Lunatic Asylum (Private)
Major J.M.T. Reilly, Fiddington House, Market Lavington, 1907

Mushroom Ketchup Maker
Hannah Smart, Dancey's Road, Atworth, 1871

Parchment Manufacturer
John Castle Cook, West Harnham, Salisbury, 1875

Peruke-maker (wigs)
Nathaniel Kington, Corsham, 1793

Razor Strop Maker
J. England, Pippett Street, Bradford on Avon, 1875

Scribbler (person who oiled and prepared yarn for carding)
Samuel Brent, Bratton, 1842

Shuttle Maker
John Keen, Shurnhold, Melksham, 1875

Snuff Grinder
Sprays Mill, Calne (for B.W. Anstie of Devizes), 1780

Staymaker (corsets)
Betty Hancock, Chippenham, 1791

Stewed Eel Shop
Frederick Wright, 8 Hill Street, Trowbridge, 1907

Tallow Chandler (& Soap Boiler)
William Speackman, Chippenham, 1822

Teazle Grower & Dealer (used for raising the nap of cloth)
Thomas James, Melksham Forest & at the Wool Pack Inn, Trowbridge, 1842

Throwster (person who twisted silk fibres into thread)
Thomas and John Ward, Crockerton, 1842

Truffle Dealer
Alfred Newton Collins, Winterslow Common, Salisbury, 1920

Turf Cutter
Amaza Gale, Box, Chippenham, 1875

Wheelwright
Benjamin Muscle, Downton, 1842

Windmill Manufacturer
John Wallis Titt & Co., Woodcock Iron Works, Warminster, 1920

MORE THAN JUST FARMING

The name of the village of Lyneham means 'linen ham', the place where flax is grown. In early times the land in this area belonged to the priory at Bradenstoke-Cum-Clack, and was a centre for the growing of flax. Other areas in Wiltshire were around Mere and Zeals.

In 1434, 1,000 rabbits were supplied to the Royal Household of Henry VI, valued at £14 (equivalent to £6,380 in 2005). Aldbourne was the most famous centre for rabbit farms (aka warrens or conigres). John Aubrey wrote in 1669 about the county's reputation for 'our famous coney-warren', producing 'the best, sweetest, and fattest (conies) of any in England'. Rabbits were bred for their meat and skins and their fur was used for hats.

There were 338 acres of woad being grown in Wiltshire in 1585 by 59 growers, dyeing being an important part of the textile industry.

'At Swindon is a quarrie of stones, excellent for paveing halls, staire-cases, &c; it being pretty white and smooth', John Aubrey wrote in his *Natural History of Wiltshire (1656–1691)*. He went on to say that it was used in some of the great houses in London such as 'Montagu-house and in Barkeley-house'.

Aubrey also noted: 'Strawberries (*fragaria*), in Colern woods, exceeding plentifull ... The poor children gather them, and sell them to Bathe; but they kill the young ashes, by barking them to make boxes to put them in.'

The Bread Stones of Great Wishford, which are set into a wall near St Giles's Church, record the fluctuating prices of wheat from 1800 (3*s*/4*d* per gall) to 2000 (£3.72 per gall).

'A liberal price will be given for any quantity of crow quills by Messrs Brodie & Dowding, stationers of Salisbury.' (*Salisbury & Winchester Journal*, June 1821)

'The newly discovered iron fields at Seend near the Bell Inn on the Melksham side, promise to produce far greater and more lucrative results than were at first anticipated. Called The Champion Iron Ore Mines they extend over 200 acres to a depth of 30 feet.' (*Salisbury & Winchester Journal*, 1856)

In 1867, Richard Jefferies wrote, 'The silk arrives here (Malmesbury) in a raw state and is unpacked in the upper storeys of the building (Archard's Mill). Much of it is Chinese, and the packages often contain small slips of paper stamped with Chinese characters. The operation of cleaning employs a large number of children who tend the machinery for that purpose.'

The *Devizes Advertiser* reported in January 1869: 'No ice having been found in sufficient quantity locally, we hear that our great bacon curers have entered into contracts for the delivery of a large quantity of ice from more northern climes, it being some years since such a delivery has taken place in Calne. This is a matter for regret, as it not only deprives the people of work of collecting the ice in a dull period of the year, but also puts the importers to a very considerable enlarged outlay.'

In Aldbourne in 1913, men were paid 2*s* 6*d* per square yard for digging flints. Women received 1*s* per square yard for picking flints up after ploughing, usually earning 8*s* a week. The flints were normally sold to the road authority for use in resurfacing highways. John Aubrey reported in 1655 that 'at Tydworth a diamond was found in a flint, which the Countess of Marleborough had set in a ring'. Ramsbury Brewery, Aldbourne, produces a beer today called Flint Knapper, a reminder of those who cut and shaped flints and, no doubt, needed a draught or two of beer to slake their thirst.

UNDER THE WEATHER, 1825

Perhaps the Medicine Warehouse, Canal, Salisbury can help. Fresh supplies of the following have just been received:

Widow Welch's Pills. This Medicine is justly celebrated for all Female Complaints, Nervous Disorders, Weakness of the Solids, Loss of Appetite, Impurity of the Blood, Relaxation by intense Heat in warm Climates. Sick Head Ache, Indigestion, Debility, Consumption, Lowness of Spirits, and particularly for all obstructions in the Female System. Mrs Smithers, Grand Daughter to the late Widow Welch, recommends Mothers, Guardians, Managers of Schools, and all those who have the care of Females of an early age, never to be without this useful medicine.

Cordial Balm of Bakasiri. This renovating Medicine affords wonderful relief in inward decays, debility, lowness of spirits, relaxation in either sex, whether hereditary or owing to youthful imprudencies; in weaknesses, tabes dorsalia, or nervous consumptions, its merits stand unrivalled; invigorating the decayed juices, and throwing a genial warmth upon the debilitated and relaxed parts that stand in need of assistance.

(*Salisbury & Winchester Journal*, 21 May 1825)

TRADING NAMES AND ASSOCIATIONS – ALAS, NO MORE!

Anglo-Bavarian Brewery Ltd (Milton Road, Swindon)

Bradley & Horningsham Depot of the National Poultry Organisation Society

Calne & District Pig Insurance Association

Colonial and American Fresh Meat Store (Silver Street, Salisbury)

Devizes Gas & Water Works & Sulphate of Ammonia

First Salisbury & District Perfect Thrift Building Society

Great Western Railway Medical Fund Society's Turkish Baths (Milton Road, Swindon)

Hampshire Down Sheep Breeders' Association (Salisbury)

London Penny Bazaar Co. Ltd (Swindon)

Marsh Gate Steam Bone Mills & Chemical Manure Co. (Stratton St Margaret)

Orphanage of Pity (Warminster)

Public Benefit Boot Company (Fore Street, Trowbridge)

Salisbury Medical Club and Provident Dispensary Club

Swindon Cold Storage & Ice Co.

Warminster Aërated Water Co.

Warminster Prosecution of Felons Society

Wessex Saddleback Pig Society (Salisbury)

Wiltshire School of Cookery & Domestic Economy (Trowbridge)

Wootton Bassett Gas, Coal, Coke & Fitting Co. Ltd

UNUSUAL NAMES IN PIGOT'S DIRECTORY, 1842

Zebulon Aldridge, baker, Wootton Bassett

Dorcas Burton, straw-hat maker and milliner, Trowbridge

Ozias Day, cheese and bacon factor, Devizes

Hollister Franklin, wheelwright, Cricklade

Quintilian Gantlett, watch and clock maker, Calne

Lazarus Hales, baker, Westbury

Enoch Hencock, baker, Chippenham

Phenis Hendy, boot and shoemaker, Bradford on Avon

Ayliff Kayns, furniture broker, Malmesbury

Keziah King, milliner, Warminster

Nimrod King, shopkeeper and salt dealer, Devizes

James Meatyard, butcher, Wilton

Mahalaleel Mead, boot and shoemaker, Bradford on Avon

Benini Mullings, cabinet maker and upholsterer, Devizes
Zaccheus Pearce, shopkeeper, Trowbridge
Ephraim Pumroy, boot and shoemaker, Wilton
Nehemiah Reed, brewer, Marlborough
Penella Shaffin, milliner and dressmaker, Salisbury
Israel Silverstone, clothes dealer, Malmesbury
Ezekial Spare, plumber, Downton
Tabitha Toogood, baker, Mere
Uriah Vines, baker, Devizes
Æneus Wingrove, stonemason, Trowbridge
Philemon Witt, publican, Five Bells, Salisbury

FRIED FISH DEALERS, 1920

Angelo Bulgarelli (Westcott Place, Swindon)
Emilio Medici (Milford Street, Swindon)
Mrs Parrott (Hythe Road, Swindon)
Paolo Stefani (Manchester Road, Swindon)
Henry Trout (Sheep Street, Devizes)

WOOL GATHERING

William Stumpe (1495–1552), clothier of Malmesbury, was instrumental in building the wool trade in the town. His looms were able to produce 3,000 rolls of broadcloth annually using wool from Cotswold Lions, a special sheep famed for its wool. The town's proximity to the important wool markets in Tetbury and Cirencester boosted its success.

In 1660 Edne Witts from Holland introduced fustian (originally a coarse cloth woven with a linen warp and cotton weft) to Aldbourne where he built up the industry, followed by Robert Wells, the Pizzle family and the Gwynnes.

'The water of this river (Avon) seems particularly qualified for the use of the clothiers; that is to say, for dying the best colours, and for fulling and dressing the cloth, so that the clothiers generally plant themselves upon this river, but especially the dyers, as at Trubridge, and Bradford, which are the two most eminent cloathing towns in that part of the vale for the making of Spanish cloths, and the nicest mixtures.' (Daniel Defoe, *Tour through the Whole of the British Isles, 1724–1728)*

'The majority of sheep are the long-legged Wiltshire breed; but many flocks consist of the South Downs sheep from Sussex, which were first introduced into the county by Mr Mighell of Kennet in 1789.' (John Britton, *The Beauties of England and Wales*, 1814)

1 September 1826, Bradford on Avon:

> I am quite convinced, not that the cloth making is at an end, but that it never will be again what it has been. Before last Christmas these manufacturers had full work, at one shilling and three pence a yard at broad-cloth weaving. They have now a quarter work, at one shilling a yard! One and three pence a yard for this weaving has been given at all times within the memory of man! Nothing can show more clearly than this, and in a stronger light, the great change which has taken place in the remuneration for labour.

(William Cobbett, *Rural Rides*, 1830)

TROWBRIDGE STREET NAMES CELEBRATING THE WOOL TRADE

Broadcloth Lane
Carders Corner
Cheviot Close
Cloth Yard
Clothier Leaze
Quilling Close
Ryeland Way

Shearman Street
Sheepcote Barton
Spinners Croft
Weavers Drive
Woolpack Meadows
Worsted Close

THREE WORK-RELATED SCULPTURES

Two Pigs, 1979, is a bronze sculpture by Richard Cowdy situated in Phelps Parade, Calne. It was unveiled four years before the closure of C&T Harris & Co., founded in 1770, famous for its Wiltshire-cured bacon, pies and sausages.

Dragonfly, 2007, a sculpture by Charlotte Moreton at Solstice Business Park services area, Amesbury, was built out of the body of a redundant Gazelle helicopter mounted on a 27ft pole. Aeronautical engineering apprentices from QinetiQ at Boscombe Down helped transform the helicopter into a work of art.

Beyond Harvest, 1990, a bronze sculpture by Colin Lambert in Cornmarket Mall, Warminster, portrays a girl sitting high up on sacks of corn gazing towards Copheap, and commemorates the days when Warminster was one of the foremost corn trading centres.

A HANDY OCCUPATION

'Gloves should be worn by a lady when out walking or driving, at tea dances, balls, dinner parties, the opera, or theatre. Men should wear gloves in the street or at a ball, when paying a call, driving, riding and in church.' (*Dictionary of Etiquette*, 1890)

In 1863, over half a million pairs of gloves valued at £61,440 were exported from Britain.

In 1851, there were fifty-five glovers listed in Ashton Keynes.

In 1871, William Boulton, master glover and inventor of the Boulton Cut Thumb, (double–stitching technique), founded Boultons Brothers, glove manufacturers at Westbury Leigh.

In 1892, the school logbook of St Mary's Primary School, Broughton Gifford, reported that attendance was poor, and one child was absent due to 'taking gloves to Holt', one of the local cottage industries.

The Ockwell family business in Cricklade produced gloves from about 1900–1994 and used to send a railway lorry load of gloves a day out of the town. After the old factory closed, the building was later converted to house the Town Council, County Branch Library and a Doctor's surgery.

Dents of Warminster made Coronation gloves for George VI and Elizabeth II, as well as gloves for the Duke of Edinburgh, Princess Anne and Zara Phillips, Prince Charles and the Duchess of Cornwall and the Queen of Norway.

Dents of Warminster produces over half a million pairs of gloves a year. Gloves are still cut by hand and it takes thirty-two different operations to manufacture a single pair.

BRATTON LIFE, 1739–41

From the diary of Jeffrey Whitaker, Schoolmaster:

1739
7 March
Rode to Warminster before Dinner. Three Rioters to be hang'd.

18 March
Dinner Rump of Beef, Bak'd pudding. Aurora Borealis, very Red & surprising in every way.

12 May
Dinner Cold Roast Beef & pancake &c. In the Afternoon carried the land and window tax to Westbury. Pd it to Rich'd Gibbs.

20 May
Dinner was a Roast Shoulder of Mutton, Bone of Bacon,

pudding &c. A great storm of Thunder, lightning & hail. Hailstones bigger than Boys marvels (marbles) with pointed ends near an Inch long.

1 June
Was extremely ill last night in the Chollick and this day an Extra bad fit sent for Dr Towgood & Dr Baily. I was bluded (14oz) & took pills in the Evening.

19 September
Made about 2 or 3 & 20 galls of cyder from falling apples. The weather continues wet.

24 September
Having a bad cold, did not go up into the school of all day. Spaniards proclaim war.

1740
22 December
Gave the poor a penny a piece. The Snow melt away apace. Rain. John Burges the small pox as thought.

23 Dec
Burges the Small pox. Snow almost gone. 4 Boys left. One of Flower's Boys taken.

1741
17 April
Finished making a Gallon of ink. This writ with it.

DAIRY PRODUCE

'Marlborough Market is Saturday: one of the greatest markets for cheese in the west of England', John Aubrey wrote in his *Natural History of Wiltshire* (1656–1691).

Daniel Defoe, in his *Tour through England and Wales (1724–1728)*, described North Wiltshire cheese: 'They make a vast quantity of that we call green cheese, which is a thin, and very soft cheese, resembling cream cheeses, only thicker, and very rich. These are brought to market new, and eaten so, and the quantity is so great, and this sort of cheese is so universally liked and accepted in London, that all the low, rich lands of this county, are little enough to supply the market.'

Wiltshire Cheese was highly prized and a valuable commodity. In February 1833, John Newcomb was found guilty at the Old Bailey of stealing 20lb of Wiltshire cheese worth 10*s* 6*d* and sentenced to seven years' transportation.

The Great Cheese Market in the Market Hall, Chippenham was reopened on 12 September 1850, following the addition of the Neeld Hall at the rear of the Town Hall.

OPENING OF THE GREAT CHEESE-MARKET, AT CHIPPENHAM, SEPTEMBER 12, 1850.—THE MARKET HALL.

November 1963, Mr Joseph Stanley Goodland of 24 Parklands, Chippenham, celebrated twenty-five years working for Bulwark Transport, Chippenham. During that time he covered 1,400 miles a week, mainly driving bulk supplies of milk from Chippenham to London. He clocked up 1.5 million miles in that time and even drove through the Blitz, finding his own routes through London to avoid the bombing.

EVERYTHING ... BUT THE SQUEAK

H. Rider Haggard, author of *She* and *King Soloman's Mine*, visited a mechanised abattoir and bacon factory in Chippenham as part of the research for his book *Being an Account of Agricultural and Social Researches in the Years 1901–02*. He described a mechanised abattoir: 'Everything is made use of except the brains – even the stomachs, which are sold for pepsine (a digestive aid). Nobody will buy pigs' brains, as the manager informed me sadly.'

In 1960, C. & T. Harris Ltd, Calne, introduced a new sausage called the 'Western Sausage' (its main ingredient being neck trimmings from chicken factories). It was heavily promoted by salesmen dressed as cowboys shooting pistols and cowgirls giving away samples. When one of the directors was asked how it was going, he replied, 'I am calling them Boomerang Sausages – they are all coming back.' The sausage was withdrawn soon after.

Arthur Bowyer started selling cured bacon and sausages from his shop in Fore Street, Trowbridge, in 1808 where he also killed and cured his own bacon out the back. By 1970, the company, now Bowyers, was one of the biggest producers of sausages and pies in the country. 'More Pork in Bowyers, tasty, tender nutritious Sausages fresh up from Wiltshire' (1962 advert). Gala Pie was one of the most popular products and Bowyer's mixers could process 5 tonnes of pork an hour and staff could boil 140,000 eggs a week.

RANDOM TRACKS

For five years (1836–1841) over 4,000 navvies worked on building the Box Tunnel, blasting their way through the two-mile stretch of Box Hill, getting through over a ton of gunpowder and a ton of candles every week. A very hazardous undertaking! A navvy would hold a 20lb drum of gunpowder under his arm and would shake some into the hole. Their only form of light in the tunnel was a candle which could gutter and spark the powder if moved. There were over 131 casualties and 100 men killed.

On 31 May 1835, the Great Western Railway Police was formed. The officer in charge, a superintendent based at Paddington, had 707 men under his command. The Great Western Railway Act (1877) was passed which gave its police officers jurisdiction on and within half a mile of the railway. It also required them to produce their Warrant card on demand with a penalty of 40s for failure to do so.

Between 1850 and 1864 the Great Western Railway Medical Fund in New Swindon provided lime for cleansing and disinfecting houses and generally supervised the health and welfare of its members.

'An ounce of care on the job is worth a ton of regret when you're crippled. Read your Rule Book. The men who compiled it were thinking of your safety. At the lowest estimate, more than a hundred men who today are reading this, as you are, will be injured, and one

ESTABLISHED 1840.

Direct Coal Supply from Colliery to Consumer. Coal, Coke, Salt, Manure, by Single Truck at Trade Prices.
DEPOT AT GREAT WESTERN RAILWAY STATION, CHIPPENHAM.

or two killed, before the end of the present month.' (From The 'Safety First' Movement, *Great Western Railway Magazine*, Nov 1913)

G.J. Churchward, Chief Engineer of the GWR (1902–1921), was killed by a train one foggy morning in 1933 while checking loose rails on the track. He was buried in the churchyard of Christ Church in Old Town, Swindon.

A 'rasher-waggon' was the common name for the roughly made frying pan in which men of the GWR steam hammer shed used to cook up a bit of bacon, an alternative to using a furnaceman's shovel (which was forbidden as heating the shovel spoiled the temper of the steel and caused it to warp). Sometimes the men roasted meat brought in for their lunch over the furnace door or on a hot lump of metal.

28 April 1929, King George V and Queen Mary visited the GWR Works during their Royal visit to Swindon. They were shown around the Carriage and Locomotive Works and met seventy-six men who all had fifty or more years' service. The King also had a go at 'driving' locomotive 4082 Windsor Castle on the Royal Train for a short distance.

The Gluepot, formerly The London Stout Tavern, in Emlyn Square, Swindon, is situated in the heart of Brunel's Railway Village. It got its name from the railway coachbuilders who used to bring their gluepots with them when they took their breaks, placing them on the central stove to keep them hot while they had a drink. The Gluepot appears in *Into the Blue, Out of the Sun* and *Never Go Back* by Robert Goddard, his character Harry Barnett's favourite drinking place. The pub owned by Hop Back Brewery serves beer that is now brewed in the former GWR Carriage Works.

A PINT OF REAL ...

Mole Catcher, Molennium, Moleo and Juliet, Holy Moley, Paddy's Tarmac Tipple, Noel Mole and Mole Lang Syne are regular and seasonal ales brewed by Moles Brewery, Bowerhill, Melksham.

Tunnel Vision, Chuffin Ale, Piston Broke, Steam Porter and Funnel Blower are beers from Box Steam Brewery, The Midlands, Holt.

Summer Lightning, Crop Circle, Elf and Hoppiness, Glass Hopper and Fuggles are beers produced by Hop Back Brewery, Downton, Salisbury.

SWEET DREAMS

'The greater part of manufacturing (in Wiltshire) consists of clothing and bedding.' (William Cobbett, *Rural Rides*, 1830)

Messrs B. Sawtells & Sons Ltd, Melksham (1902–1990), later known as The West of England Bed, Feathers & Down Purifying Co.

H. Chapman & Co., founded in Trowbridge by Hedley Chapman in 1871, started by making straw palliasses selling at 3s 6d a pair, moving on to mattresses using the flock by-product from the local woollen industry. In the 1930s, with the arrival of interior sprung mattresses, they expanded to become Airsprung in 1951. The current Canal Road site is the largest single-site furniture manufacturer in the UK. Their 2012 king-size Airsprung Ortho Trizone mattress 'containing a 12.5 gauge spring unit, providing extra support in the centre lumber region' sells for £225 – a far cry from its straw predecessor.

6

LEISURE TIME

ALL SORTS OF FUN

Nuns' Knees-Up

The Accounts for the Order of the Benedictine Nuns at Wilton Abbey showed the extra food ordered for the Great Feast held between 13 September and St Edith's Day, 16 September 1299, to celebrate the appointment of the new abbess, Emma La Blonde:

16 swans	60 gallons milk
13 peacocks	2 casks wine
13 partridges	2,550 eggs bought
3 boars	27 quarters of malt used for beer

A Good Night's Sleep

Samuel Pepys visited Marlborough on 15 June 1668, staying at The (White) Hart, 'a good house'. He recorded sleeping so well and long after a supper and 'musique whose innocence pleased me ... so as all the five coaches that come this day from Bath, as well as we, were gone out of the town before six'.

Eating Well

Jane Austen stayed at The Bear Hotel, Devizes, on 16 May 1799, on her way to Bath with her nieces. She wrote to her sister Cassandra: 'At Devizes we had comfortable rooms and a good dinner, to which we sat down about five; amongst other things we had asparagus and a lobster, which made me wish for you, and some cheesecakes, on which the children made so delightful a supper as to endear the town of Devizes to them for a long time.'

Rustic Sports

'Peter's Finger Inn, Salisbury, on 18 June 1821 being the anniversary
of the Battle of Waterloo, there will be a match of single-stick* played
for a good OLD cheese, wrestling for a Beaver Hat; Girls' running for
Ribbons; jumping in sacks; with various other amusements.'

(Salisbury & Winchester Journal)

*single-stick or backswording was a violent game between two men,
each with a big stick and one hand tied to their side. Rules dictated
that the blood must flow an inch from some part of the head before
either party is declared victor.

More Rustic Sports

Games on offer at the Hungerford Revel, Wilts 1826 included:

Climbing a greasy pole for a piece of bacon
Old women drinking hot tea for snuff
Racing between twenty and thirty old women for a pound of tea
Grinning through horse-collars
Hunting a pig with a soaped tail

Tightrope Walking in Wilton

Jean François Gravelet, aka Charles Blondin, tightrope walker, visited
Wiltshire in 1873. Famous as the first person to walk across Niagara
Falls on a tightrope, he was touring Europe and the United Kingdom,
and brought his tightrope act to a paying crowd of between 20,000
and 25,000 at Wilton Park. Poet Edward Slow recorded the event in a
Wiltshire dialect poem:

... Zo quick his nimble legs did go,
They kept time to the band below;
An then to ael tha vokes zurprise,
He tied a bandage roun his eyes.
An ael his head an half his back,
He put into a girt thick zack;
An once agean took pole in han,
An tried upon tha rope ta stan.
Pretendin two ar dree times ta slip,
Bit that wur ael a bit a flip;
Var on a went as blind a bat,
An steady as a mouse or cat...
(Blondin at Wilton Park, Bank Holiday 4 August 1873)

Fancy Dress Skating Carnival, 1910
'Premier Rink, Trowbridge
The Skating Rink's the place for pleasure
Rolling round to music's measure.
Many hours of pure delight
Eleven at morn' till twelve midnight'

First-Class Fun
Passengers travelling on the Great Western Railway could pass the time with a GW jigsaw bought from a station bookstall. The first of a series of 44 jigsaws was of Engine No. 4073 Caerphilly Castle, produced especially for the British Empire Exhibition at Wembley in 1924 where the locomotive was on display. The 150-piece jigsaw was on sale for 5s.

Carnival Time
The Avon India Rubber Co. float won first prize in the 1928 Melksham Carnival and went on to win third prize at Trowbridge Carnival. The tableau was emblazoned with the slogan 'Tyres from bladders were derived. Our tyres go on though pigs have died'.

Red Carpet Treatment
On 29 November 1937, rising British film star Margaret Lockwood accompanied the Countess of Radnor to the opening of the New Gaumont Cinema, Trowbridge, on the old Palace site in Fore Street. The first show was *King Solomon's Mines*, starring Paul Robeson, and *Oh Doctor!* with Edward Everett Horton.

Stones at Longleat
The Rolling Stones performed at the 3rd Pop Festival at Longleat House, 2 August 1964, before a crowd of 16,000. They were supported by Danny Clarke and The Jaguars, and Tony Rivers and The Castaways. Admission was 2/6d and the band was paid £1,000.

Gardening Duties
Roddy Llewellyn, son of 1950s Olympic medal show-jumper Sir Harry Llewellyn, was head gardener at the 47-acre Surrendell Farm, Hulllavington, in the 1970s where he regularly entertained his friend Princess Margaret, at what became known as a hippie commune.

Seeing Circles
The Wiltshire Crop Circle Study Group has been producing calendars since 1996, featuring the best local formations of each year with landscape views, overhead and groundshots, and diagrams. It is

'designed to bring the wonder of the phenomenon as it unfolds in Wiltshire into your living space'. More than 6,000 crop circles have been documented since 1980.

... AND A DISASTER

Up in the Air

Apart from his work as MP for Malmesbury, Walter Powell (1842–1881) is also remembered for his ballooning exploits and his death as a result of a hot air balloon accident. He once flew from the Cross Hayes where gas from the Malmesbury Gas Works was piped into his balloon Eclipse, which made a short trip passing over Lea and Somerford, finally landing at Spirthill. His last flight was with two companions on 10 December 1881 in the balloon Saladin, to make meteorological observations. They took off from Bath but over Dorset got into trouble, managing to bring the balloon down near Chesil Beach. When the basket hit the ground, the two men got out, along with some ballast. Powell stayed in but the now lighter balloon took off again out to sea, never to be seen again. The story was big news, with reported sightings from as far afield as Scotland and Spain. There is a memorial tablet to Powell in St John the Baptist Church, Little Somerford Church.

SPORTING SNAPSHOTS

Cricket

Sir Arthur Conan Doyle, creator of Sherlock Holmes, played for the Marylebone Cricket Club (MCC) against Wiltshire at Trowbridge Cricket Club Ground on 24 July 1899 in a two-day match. A few days before, Doyle wrote to his mother: 'I play for the MCC against Wiltshire at Trowbridge, an awfully difficult place to get at. However, it is the first county match the MCC had asked me for and I felt I ought to go.' The MCC fielded a side of mixed pros and amateurs against Wiltshire and were easily beaten by an innings and 86 runs. Doyle's comments about Trowbridge's inaccessibility came true as he was late and missed the MCC's first innings.

Allan Gibson 'AG' Steel (1858–1914), one of seven cricketing brothers, was a Lancashire and England player, said to be the equal of the legendary W.G. Grace. He went to Marlborough College, where he began his cricketing career in 1874 when he got his place in the Marlborough Eleven. In 1884, he made his highest Test score of 148, which was the first test-match century ever scored at Lord's. He was a member of the MCC (1880–1890) and its president in 1902.

Clifford Bax (1886–1962), poet, playwright and author of a biography of W.G. Grace (1952) lived at the Manor House, Broughton Gifford. He organised summer 'cricket weeks' (1911 to around 1933 – apart from the war years) with a circle of friends, including poet Edward Thomas, playwright Herbert Farjeon, Jungian pyschoanalyst Godwin Baynes and his composer brother Arnold, playing local teams from surrounding villages.

In the 11 to 29 August 1932 tour they played Chippenham, Grittleton, Melksham, Lansdown, Bruton, Lacock, Frome, County Mental Hospital, Devizes and Corsham.

Racing Tips
Fred Darling was master of Beckhampton Stables near Marlborough (1914–1947) and trained winners of 19 Classics including 7 Derby winners. In 1932, Gordon Richards began riding for Darling, clocking up 259 wins, beating the record previously held by Fred Archer since 1885.

In 1942, Princess Elizabeth was taken by her parents to Beckhampton Stables near Marlborough to watch her father King George VI's horses Big Gun and Sun Chariot train. Current owner Roger Charlton is now trainer to the Queen. Four of her horses – Moidore, Border Legend, Dawn Glory and Candaluminescence – are in training there.

Thoroughbred horse trainer Alec Taylor Jnr (1862–1943) followed in the footsteps of this father, Alec Snr, at Manton Stud, near Marlborough, one of the finest training centres of its time. Also known as the Wizard of Manton, Alec Jnr won 21 Classics including Ascot Gold Cup (1909 and 1918) and a dozen trainers' championships. Favourite horse Gainsborough was a Triple Crown winner (2000 Guineas, Derby and St Leger) in 1918, ridden by French jockey, Joseph Childs, who became first jockey to King George V in 1925.

John Lawrence, Lord Oaksey (1929 –2012), horse racing journalist and television presenter, of Oaksey near Malmesbury, was a steeplechase jockey with over 200 winners, including 11 Grand National rides (1961–1975) and second place in the 1963 Grand National on Carrickbeg. In 1964, he became a founding trustee of the Injured Jockeys Fund, before becoming its president. His father, Lord Justice Geoffrey Lawrence, presided at the Nuremburg Trials (1945–1946) which John Oaksey attended when he was sixteen.

Motor Racing

Castle Combe Circuit opened in 1950 on the former RAF airfield, the circuit following the perimeter of the old air base. It is one of the longest established circuits in the UK. In 1955, the only International Formula One race ever to be held in Wiltshire at Castle Combe was won by Harry Schell.

Six Racing Legends at Castle Combe

Stirling Moss won his heat and final in October 1952 in his 500cc Cooper Norton Formula 3 car.
John Surtees won 500cc motorcycle in 1952.
Mike Hailwood won 250cc race on legendary 250cc Honda Four in 1962
Barry Sheene won 125cc motorcycle race 1972.
Nigel Mansell won Formula Ford race in 1976.
Ayrton Senna won Formula Ford in 1982.

The Hon. Mrs Victor Bruce [*née* Mildred Petre] (1895–1990) lived in Bradford on Avon from 1950 until her death. The *Ceylon Observer* of 6 Sept 1927 reported:

MOTORING IN ARCTIC EUROPE
Two British motorists who have just achieved the feat of breaking the 'farthest North' record in a motor car, were turned back when 270 miles within the Arctic Circle by swampy conditions, arising from the intense heat. The Hon Mrs Victor Bruce and party (husband and Mr Beare) returned to London after a 6,000 mile trip through Northern Europe to Finland and Lapland. They averaged 200 miles a day for 28 days. Mrs Bruce was undertaking a survey of roads in Sweden for the Automobile Association.

In 1929, she achieved the world record for single-handedly driving a super-charged 4.5 litre Bentley at Montlhéry for twenty-four hours, averaging 89mph, a mark which has never been surpassed by a woman.

Sporting Stars

Martin Ashby, Swindon Speedway Champion, was born in Marlborough in 1944, and represented Swindon Robins (1961–1967 and 1971–1980). He reached the final of the Speedway World Championship in 1968.

  Record appearances: 641.
  Rides: 2,692.
  Points total: 5476.5.

Nick 'Bang Bang' Blackwell, boxer, was born in Trowbridge and attended John of Gaunt School. He became the youngest middleweight English champion, aged twenty, with a victory against York's Harry Matthews on 20 November 2010.

New Zealander Barry 'Briggo' Briggs became the first (and only) man to win the World Speedway Championship in Gothenburg, Sweden, on 11 September 1964 while riding with Swindon Robins. He went on to win again in 1966.

Rugby player Will Carling, British and Irish Lions and Harlequins and England Captain (1988–1996) was born in Bradford on Avon. He was the youngest man ever to hold the position of captain aged twenty-two, leading one of the most successful sides in English rugby history.

Phil Crump, aka 'Marathon Man', one of Swindon Speedway's all-time greats, was born in Mildura, Victoria, Australia. He rode in three World Finals and won four Australian Championships. He represented Swindon (1979–1986 & 1990) and won the Blunsdon-staged *Evening Advertiser* Superstar Individual Event in 1982 and 1984. He made 1,855 rides with Swindon.

Walter Goodall George (1858–1943), athlete, record-breaking mile-runner and Victorian superstar, was born in Calne. He did much of his early training on Cherhill Downs, often running with the Beaufort Hunt. On 23 August 1886 at Lillie Bridge Athletics Ground, George ran the mile in 4 mins 12.75 secs, breaking the world record. A memorial plaque on Calne Town Hall was unveiled in 1986 by Sydney Wooderson, the next British runner to achieve the fastest time in 1935.

W·G·GEORGE
RUNNER
I MILE, 4 MIN.- 12¾ SEC.

David Hemery, athlete and Olympic hurdler, won Gold at the 1968 Mexico City Games for 400m, Silver in 1972 at Munich, and Silver in 1969 at Athens, lives at Fyfield near Marlborough.

James Kibblewhite (1866–1941), athlete, was born in Purton and worked as a machinist in the Swindon GWR Works. He began his athletics career in 1884 and won many medals over the next ten years, breaking the 3-mile English record and world record in London. Kibblewhite Close and a room at The Pear Tree Hotel, Purton, are named after him.

Stephen Lee, professional snooker player, ranked no. 5 in the world 2000/01 and 2003/04, was born in Trowbridge where he still lives.

Shelley-Marie Rudman, Olympic skeleton bobsleigh medallist was born in Swindon and has her home in Pewsey. She won Silver in Turin, 2006, was European Champion in 2009, Olympic team Captain in Vancouver, 2010, and World Cup Overall Silver medallist 2009/10.

Bruce Tulloh, champion long-distance runner, well-known for running barefoot, set new British and European records for Two Miles, Three Miles and Six Miles and competed in 2 European, 2 Commonwealth and one Olympic Games. He won Gold in the 5000m at the 1962 European Championships. He taught Biology at Marlborough College for twenty years and lives in West Stowell near Pewsey.

2012 Olympians

Laura Bechtolsheimer from Oaksey, who attended St Mary's School, Calne, won Team Gold and Individual Bronze in dressage at the 2012 London Olympics on her horse Alf (Mistral Højris).

Ed McKeever, aka the Kayak King, from Bradford on Avon, won Gold in the 2012 London Olympics in the K1 200m kayak final at Eton Dorney on 11 August 2012. This was the first time the sport had been in the Olympics. Ed attended St Laurence School and joined Bradford on Avon Rowing Club in 1987 when he was twelve.

Stephanie Milward, swimmer and the most prolific medallist at 2012 London Paralympics with four Silver medals and a Bronze, was awarded the freedom of Corsham Town, where she grew up and went to school.

Heather Stanning, Captain, 3–2 Regiment Royal Artillery, who was born in Yeovil in 1985, was based at Larkhill Camp when she won Gold in the 2012 London Olympics in the women's coxless rowing pairs with team-mate Helen Glover at Eton Dorney on 8 August 2012.

Sarah Storey, swimmer and cyclist, who lives in Tidworth, won Gold in the 2012 London Paralympics in 3km C5 individual event.

Dead Before His Time

The Times mistakenly published the obituary of William Grenfell, 1st Baron Desborough (1855–1945), MP for Salisbury (1880–1882 and 1885–1886), on 2 December 1920, having confused him with Lord Bessborough. Grenfell was a member and then President of the Bartitsu Club (aka Bartitsu Academy of Arms and Physical Culture) a gentleman's club in London, which practised an early form of martial arts, the 'New Art of Self Defence', pioneered by E.W. Barton-Wright. He won a silver medal for fencing at the 1906 'Second International Olympic Games in Athens' and was President of the 1908 London Olympiad. His three sons died before him and his title became extinct on his death.

'THE ROBINS': SWINDON TOWN FC MISCELLANY

Beer Up

In 1896, brewer Thomas Arkell made a loan of £300 to Swindon Town club to build its first stand on the Wiltshire County Ground. Thus began a long association between club and brewery. Away fans today are located in the Arkells (formerly North) Stand, completed in August 1971, which can house 1,200 fans.

Red Devil

Fleming Way in Swindon is named after Harold Fleming (1887–1955) who was born in Downton and played for Swindon Town FC (1907–1924). He was capped nine times for England, the only player to play for England while at Swindon. He was the second highest all-time scorer, with 204 goals. Harry Morris was first with 229 goals and Don Rogers third with 181.

The *Swindon Advertiser* wrote about Fleming's performance in the 1910 Dubonnet Cup match in Paris: 'We saw yesterday one of the best, if not the best, forwards in England, Fleming, 'the Red Devil', who was astounding. His play excited the enthusiasm of the crowd. His first goal was a marvellous one.' A bronze statue of Fleming by Carlton Attwood stands in the club's foyer. After his retirement he ran a sports shop in Commercial Road until his death.

Wartime Hero

Yorkshire-born footballer Alan 'Foxie' Fowler (1911–1944) signed for Leeds United at age sixteen and went to Swindon Town FC in 1934. He scored a hat-trick against Luton in 1935 in the first six minutes of the game – a record time. He was ranked 12th in all-time scorers, with 102 gaols in 224 appearances. He was serving with The Dorsets, part of the 43rd Wessex Division, when he died during a massive bombardment of enemy positions at Normandy, 10 July 1944; sadly, as the result of friendly fire from RAF Typhoons which had dropped their bombs in their area.

No Play
The War Office requisitioned the County Ground for use as a prisoner of war camp, and huts were erected on the pitch in 1940. New manager Neil Harris was just three games into his first season when all matches stopped; he died shortly after.

Hail to the Player
The star-studded All Stars XI, including Don Revie, Tom Finney, Stanley Matthews, Billy Wright, Bobby Moore and Tommy Docherty, took part in a testimonial match for Maurice Owen on 9 April 1962. Owen played for Swindon Town (1947–1963), making 601 appearances and scoring 165 goals. He died in July 2000.

Crying Shame
Stuart Mac, BBC *Wiltshire Sound* reporter, was so upset at the 7–0 defeat in the away game Bolton Wanderers v Swindon match on 8 March 1997 that he couldn't stop crying on air as he described the goals in his post match summary. He had to be taken off air.

Record Number of League Appearances Made for One Club
John Trollope (left back) turned out for the Town in 770 games between 1960 and 1980, an achievement which was rewarded with an MBE.

Sold
A rare copy of a Swindon Town football programme from the division three match against Thames AFC on 27 September 1930 was sold for £400 in September 2012 at Lockdales Auctioneer in Ipswich. Also, 90 Swindon programmes from 1910 to 1945 went under the hammer earlier in the year, raising £9,861.

OTHER FOOTIE

Chippenham Town was host to The Original TV All Stars XI v The Ivy Inn XI, Heddington Charity Match on 26 February 1961. A crowd of nearly 3,000 attended the match at Hardenhuish Park and saw the 7–5 victory by the TV All Stars, which included Mike and Bernie Winters (Captain – who scored four goals), Jess Conrad and Bernard Bresslaw.

Two Trowbridge Stars

W. George of Trowbridge Town, a serving soldier in the Royal Artillery at Trowbridge Barracks, was goalkeeper for Trowbridge Town in the mid-1890s. He was spotted at a match between Trowbridge and Reading and was signed up with Aston Villa in 1897. He went on to play for England in 1901 against Germany and in 1902 against Scotland, Wales and Ireland. He won a Cup Final medal in the 1904/05 season playing for Villa against Newcastle United at Crystal Palace.

Trowbridge Town drew 4–4 in a friendly match against Tottenham Hotspur on 31 January 1959 before a crowd of 3,000. In the Spurs team was Danny Blanchflower, captain of Ireland, wing half for Spurs, Footballer of the Year, and chairman of the Professional Footballers' Association, as well as being a popular TV personality at that time.

CLUBS & SOCIETIES – ALAS, NO MORE!

Bradford on Avon Poultry Society
British Railways Staff Association Brass and Silver Jubilee Band (Swindon)
Chippenham Amateur Tobacco Growers Association
Comrades of the Great War (Ludgershall)
Fisherton Progressive & Radical Club (Salisbury)
Malmesbury Dorcas Society (for the relief of the poor)
Marlborough Reading and Mutual Improvement Society
Mere Down Coursing Club
The Patriots' Society (Lacock)
Piscatorial Society (Swindon)
Salisbury Microscopical Society
Sons of Temperance Friendly & Approved Society, Mere
Sutton Benger Harmonic Society
Trowbridge Foot Beagles
Trowbridge Histrionic Club
Trowbridge Mandoline Band
United Ancient Order of Druids (Swindon)
Wiltshire Auxiliary British & Foreign Bible Society (Devizes)
Wootton Bassett and District Chrysanthemum and Caged Bird Society

WHAT YOU CAN JOIN IN 2013

Ali Barbers Barbershop Harmony Club (Salisbury)
Appalachian Folk Step (Corsham)
Avago Karting and Laser Shooting (West Dean)
Camcorder Club Zoom (Swindon)
Citroen2CV Club (Association of Snails) (Swindon)
Debutots Early Years Drama (Swindon)
Flying Druids Model Aircraft Club (Salisbury)
Great Bustard Morris (Swindon)
Grecophiles' Social Club (Melksham)
Haunch of Venison Mountain Rescue Club (Salisbury)
Hips and Haws (clog dancing (Chippenham)
Jung Shin Kwan Hapkido (Salisbury)
Manaraefan Vikings (re-enactmen (Salisbury)
Oi Sambistas Samba Band (Devizes)
SADGITS (Salisbury And District Grand International Transmitting Society)
Sahara Sisters Belly Dancing (Chippenham)
Sarum Hobnob Lacemakers (Salisbury)
Swindon UFO Research
Swindon Ukulele Club
Tisbury Twisters (trampolining)
Wiltshire Tortoise Group

SCHOOL'S OUT

School logbooks show that many Wiltshire schools took time off to allow children to visit shows such as Barnum & Bailey's Circus and Wombwell's Menagerie (later Wombwell & Bostock's), or to watch them pass by, like the pupils at The National School in Avebury did in March 1890: 'Kennet and Beckhampton children stayed away to see Wombell's Menagerie pass by on the main road to on its way to Calne'. Trowbridge boys sadly missed out on the show on 6 May 1913: 'School closed at 3.30 so that boys could visit Wombwell's and Bostock's Menagerie which did not turn up due to a mishap at Calne'.

HAVING YOUR CAKE ... AND EATING IT!

The annual Great Western Railway Children's Fete organised by the Mechanics' Institute since 1868, took place at the GWR Park (former Cricket Field) in Faringdon Road, Swindon. In 1890 over 20,000 people attended and in 1904, up to 38,000. By the 1920s the Fete was serving four tons of cake, and an automated cake-cutting machine had been specially designed and built in the Swindon Works. The lady helpers became adept at bagging a slice along with a free roundabout ticket for each child. The Swindon Co-operative Provident Society bakery in Henry Street took over the work in the mid-1920s. In 1939, the price of a cup of tea and a slice of cake was 3*d*, and children had to bring their own cup.

GIVE ME THE MONEY

The Ferguson Gang was a group of anonymous philanthropic bluestockings in the late 1930s, which raised money towards the preservation of houses and land for the National Trust, including Avebury. The women wore masks and assumed false names to hide their identity as they handed over bags of silver they had collected to the National Trust. They raised over £4,500 (equivalent to £130,000 in 2005). Only one member, Dr Margaret Stueart-Pollard, a great-niece of Gladstone, was officially outed in her *Times* obituary in 1996.

UNUSUAL HOBBY, 1955

From the *Westinghouse Review*: 'Fred Parsonson, Chief Draughtsman of the Signal Drawing Office at Westinghouse, London, moved to Chippenham in 1939 when the Sales and Engineering Departments were evacuated from the City. In addition to making wooden toys, dolls' houses and model shops in his spare time he also grew and cured his own tobacco. He was so successful that he produced an average yield of 12lbs a year (more than a year's supply for the average smoker). He was Chairman of the Chippenham Amateur Tobacco Growers Association.'

FOURTEEN UNUSUAL TOWN TWINNINGS

Avoca, Ireland	Bromham
Caln Township, Pennsylvania, US	Calne
Chattanooga, Tennessee, US	Swindon
Elblag, Poland	Trowbridge
Gunjur, The Gambia	Marlborough
Malmesbury, South Africa	Malmesbury
Marlborough, New Zealand	Marlborough
Ocotal, Nicaragua	Swindon
Oamaru, New Zealand	Devizes
Oujda, Morocco	Trowbridge
Salisbury, Maryland, US	Salisbury
Salisbury, North Carolina, US	Salisbury
Tornio, Finland	Devizes
Toruń, Poland	Swindon
Walt Disney World, Florida, US	Swindon

BACKSTAGE DYNASTY

The Garrison Theatre in Tidworth, a rare survivor of a purpose-built garrison theatre, has been managed by members of the Pickernell family since it opened in 1909. Herbert Pickernell, former stage manager of the Empire in Swindon, came over from the theatre with owner Alfred Manners. The first event held was a boxing tournament played to a full house (capacity 1,700 standing), in which the winner of the final bout received £10 and the loser £5. The theatre was used for all kinds of entertainment from ballet to Big Bands over the years, and during the Second World War many international stars, such as James Cagney, Bob Hope and Will Hay, came to entertain the troops here.

ROOT TROUBLE

The Ancient Order of Sherston Mangold Hurlers holds its Annual Mangold Hurl on Sherston Village Green every October since its revival in 2006. The traditional game consists of contestants standing with both feet in a pitching basket and hurling a mangold (mangel-wurzel) at the 'Norman' – a large leafless mangold which acts as the target. Sadly, the 2012 contest was cancelled due to a lack of mangolds.

7

INVENTORS, PIONEERS & SCHOLARS

FLYING MONK

Eilmer of Malmesbury was a Benedictine monk, born about 980, best known for his attempt at flying in around 1005. Wearing a pair of homemade wings attached to his arms and feet he took off from the top of the Malmesbury Abbey tower, covering a distance of about 200 metres before coming down with a bump into a marshy field (now known as St Aldhelm's Meadow) breaking both legs. Thanks to historian William of Malmesbury, we know all this. He also recorded Eilmer's sightings of Halley's Comet, first as a boy in 989 and again in 1066.

FLYING MONK

LEVIATHAN MAN

Thomas Hobbes of Malmesbury (1588–1679), philosopher and author of *Leviathan*, was born in Westport, Malmesbury, where his father was a curate. He was educated at Oxford and travelled widely. He wrote *Leviathan* or *The Matter, Forme and Power of A Commonwealth Ecclesiasticall and Civil* (1651) while in exile as a Royalist in Paris with the court of Charles II. The illustrated front cover was designed by Hobbes and probably represents him, although it also looks like Charles I and Oliver Cromwell. Hobbes stated that the natural state of mankind (the state before a central government is formed) as a 'warre of every man against every man', resulting in the life of man being 'solitary, poore, nasty, brutish, and short'. He died at Hardwick Hall, Derbyshire.

ARCHITECT OF LONDON

Sir Christopher Wren (1632–1723) mathematician, astronomer and architect of St Paul's Cathedral (1666–1674), was born in a cottage at the bottom of Wise Lane, East Knoyle, where his father was rector at St Marys. Wren was responsible for the design of over fifty new churches after the Great Fire of London, and other buildings such as the Observatory and The Royal Naval College Greenwich, Trinity College Library in Cambridge, and the façade of Hampton Court Palace. He was buried in the crypt of St Paul's Cathedral. An inscribed wall tablet nearby reads: *Si monumentum requiris, circumspice* – 'If you seek his memorial, look about you'.

UNDERSTANDING THE BRAIN

Dr Thomas Willis (1621–1675), physician, neuroanatomist and one of the founders of the Royal Society, was born in Great Bedwyn. He was the first person to recognise a number of illnesses including diabetes, coining the term *diabetes mellitus* (the Latin word for honey – which relates to the sweet nature of the urine of people with diabetes), akathisia (restless legs syndrome) and the symptoms of malaria. The Circle of Willis (*circulus arteriosus cerebri*) is a circle of arteries that sits at the base of the brain and is named after him. His most famous book was on the anatomy of the brain, *Cerebri Anatome* (1664) declaring the brain to be 'the chief seat of the Rational Soul in a man ... and as the chief mover in the animal Machine'. He introduced the new concept of a neurological basis to the bodily functions and is regarded as the father of neuroscience, coining the word 'neurology'.

SWEET SUCCESS

Joseph Fry (1728–1787), doctor, chocolate manufacturer and type founder, was born in Sutton Benger. He was the son of a Quaker shopkeeper and after apprenticeship to an apothecary and doctor, set up his own business in Bristol in 1753. He began selling chocolate (always a good alternative drink to beer for teetotallers) and went into business with John Vaughan when he bought a local chocolate business. Within three years Fry, Vaughan & Co. had agents in fifty–three towns, with chocolate works in Bristol and a warehouse in London. Fry left the business to his sons so he could become a type founder – starting the Fry Letter Foundry with partner William Pine, printer of the *Bristol Gazette*. By 1847, his great-grandson had discovered a way to mix some of the melted cacao butter back into defatted or 'Dutched' cocoa powder (mixed with sugar) to create a paste which could be pressed into a mould. And so the chocolate bar was invented!

GREEN MATTERS

Jan Ingen Housz FRS (1730–1799), Dutch physician, biologist and chemist, was a regular guest at Bowood House, Calne, in the 1790s until his death there. He was buried in a vault under St Mary's Church, Calne. As a result of successfully inoculating members of the Habsburg family in Vienna against smallpox in 1768, he became private counsellor and personal physician to Emperor Joseph II son of Empress Maria Theresa. His real genius was in demonstrating, in England, in 1779, that green plant materials, especially leaves, release oxygen (and so 'cleanse' the air) but only in direct sunlight, the process now known as photosynthesis.

THE BREATH OF LIFE

Joseph Priestley FRS (1733–1804), theologian and scientist, was employed by Lord Shelburne (later Marquess of Lansdowne) at Bowood House near Calne between 1773 and 1780, and in London as his intellectual companion and librarian. Priestley lived briefly at No. 19, The Green, Calne, and then at the Old Vicarage in Anchor Road. On 1 August 1774, while working in his Bowood 'laboratory', Priestley used sunlight focused through a convex lens (a 'burning' lens) to ignite some mercuric oxide. He found that the gas released had amazing properties. This was the first isolation of what we now call oxygen. Along with other contemporaries, he demonstrated that atmospheric air is a mixture of several elemental gases. Priestley also held vigorously non-conformist religious beliefs and these, with his support of the French Revolution, put his life at jeopardy in the notorious reactionary riots in Birmingham in 1791, forcing his emigration to America, where he died.

FREEDOM

George Bourne (1780–1845), founder of the American Anti–Slavery Society and editor and co-owner of the *Baltimore Daily Gazette*, was born in Westbury and emigrated to Virginia, USA, in 1810. He also wrote biographies of Revd John Wesley, Napoleon Bonaparte and Thomas Jefferson and anti-slavery articles for the *Christian Intelligencer*.

RUBBER MEN

Thomas Hancock (1786–1865), inventor responsible for founding the rubber industry in this country, was born and educated in Marlborough. He was working with his brother Walter as a coachbuilder and began experimenting with raw natural latex, looking for ways to waterproof fabrics to protect passengers on their coaches. Hancock took out sixteen patents all relating to rubber (1820–1847), including the masticator, a machine which shredded rubber scraps, allowing rubber to be recycled after being formed into blocks or rolled into sheets. Hancock started supplying Macintosh with his masticated rubber in 1830. He patented elastic fastenings for gloves, suspenders, shoes and stockings. In 1843 after seeing some specimens of 'cured' rubber by Charles Goodyear at an exhibition in London, he filed a patent for the 'vulcanisation of rubber'. Eventually

Hancock became a partner in the firm of Charles Macintosh & Co., though he still carried on his own business in London.

Brother Walter Hancock (1799–1852) also invented steamed-powered road vehicles. One of his steam omnibuses, the Enterprise, ran between Paddington and the Bank in London.

THE SOURCE OF THE NILE

John Hanning Speke (1827–1864), soldier and explorer, was born in Devon but died aged thirty-seven at Neston Park near Corsham as the result of a shooting accident on the estate of relative, George Fuller. Speke was the first European to reach Lake Victoria in East Africa in 1858, on an expedition with Richard Burton who contracted malaria and had to turn back. He was the first to identify it as the source of the Nile after a second expedition in 1862. He published *Journal of the Discovery of the Source of the Nile* in 1863.

GONE TO EARTH

Reverend Henry Moule (1801–1880), clergyman and inventor of the dry earth closet, was born in Melksham, educated at Marlborough Grammar School and ordained in Melksham in 1823. He was a vicar in Gillingham, Dorset, when he became concerned about the health of his parishioners and their unsanitary living conditions, which led to diseases such as cholera. He believed that it was better for human waste to return to the soil rather than be flushed from the water closets into rivers. 'In God's providence there is no waste. And it was never meant that even the privy-soil or sink-water, or the water of slop-bucket should be wasted. Still less that they should poison fresh air, and produce sickness.' He patented his commode design in 1860, in partnership with James Bannehr. The earth closet proved successful, especially in hospitals, military camps, and in India, and he was

Moule's Earth Closet, 1860

credited with helping to improve the health of millions of people around the world.

FATHER OF PHOTOGRAPHY

William Henry Fox Talbot (1800–1877), pioneering photographer, botanist, mathematician, astronomer and MP for Chippenham (1832–1834), was born at Melbury House, Dorset. He lived at Lacock Abbey between 1827 and 1877, and is buried in Lacock village cemetery. He discovered the negative/positive photographic process in 1835. His first camera negative was of the lattice window at Lacock Abbey. He patented the calotype process in 1841, going on to develop the three primary elements of photography: developing, fixing, and printing. He was also one of the few men in Britain able to read cuneiform having worked on finds from Ninevah at the British Museum. He published translations of inscriptions by Assyrian Kings, some of whose palaces had been discovered in 1847. As MP he presented a petition on the impact of the poor laws in Lacock and he supported railway expansion into the West Country. A life-size statue of Fox Talbot sculpted by Greta Berlin stands in Greenway Business Park, Chippenham.

TROWBRIDGE SHORTHAND BROTHERS: HOME AND ABROAD

Isaac Pitman (1813–1897) was born in Timbrell Street, Trowbridge. He was a teacher, publisher and inventor of a system of phonetic shorthand, the Stenographic Sound Hand, later known as Pitman's Shorthand. He was the third of eleven children of Samuel Pitman, overseer of a weaving factory. He trained to be a teacher in London and originally taught Taylor's shorthand to his pupils but decided to work on a new method which was based on the sounds of a language. His *Stenographic Sound Hand* was published in 1837, and by the 1890s it was part of the school curriculum and estimated that 100,000 people a year learned the system. He founded the Phonetics Institutes and set up Pitman Publishing. A resident of Bath for fifty-eight years, he was knighted in 1894 and died at his home, No. 17 Royal Crescent, Bath.

Benjamin 'Benn' Pitman (1822–1910) was born in Trowbridge and emigrated to America in 1853 to promote older brother Isaac's shorthand system. He became known as the 'Father of Phonetic

Shorthand in America'. He trained as an architect, worked in the printing business and invented the electroplating process of relief engraving in 1855. He served as a Captain in an Ohio regiment on the Union side in the Civil War and went on to study woodcarving. He established the woodcarving department at the University of Cincinnati School of Design, where he taught and played a significant role in the American Arts and Crafts Movement (1873–1892) and in promoting women's work. He led the five-man team of recorders for the Lincoln assassination trial (1865) and published *The Assassination of President Lincoln and the Trial of the Conspirators* (1867) and a biography of his brother Isaac (1902). Benn Pitman House, the home he built (1880–1884) in Cincinnati, Ohio, full of his artistic woodcarvings, is a registered historic building.

EASY PLOUGHING

John Fowler (1826–1864) of Melksham invented the mechanical plough to solve the problem of large amounts of land that he saw left uncultivated due to poor drainage. An engineer by training he decided that the answer lay in a mole. Not the furry kind, of course, but a mechanical plough that dug drainage ditches into which drainage pipes could be laid. It replaced the horse–drawn plough with a horse–powered engine. In 1852 he invented a steam driven plough, which proved popular around the world, bringing uncultivated land into production.

BLOOMING WONDERFUL

James Lye (1830–1906), gardener, pioneering fuchsia breeder and award-winning potato grower (1886, new variety 'Clipper'), was born in Market Lavington. Apprenticed at twelve to his father who was head gardener at Clyffe Hall, he took over the same position eleven years later working for the Hon. Mrs Louisa Hay (*née* Pleydell-Bouverie). Fuchsias were very popular in Victorian times and gardeners in large houses and estates wanted impressive displays for their drives and grounds. Lye developed and perfected the art of growing pillar (pyramid) fuchsias, 8-10ft high and 5ft across at the base. He was known as 'Champion Fuchsia Grower in the West of England' (1866). He developed over ninety-four cultivars (1860–1901), many of which are still grown today, such as Coachman, Pink Pearl and Lye's Unique.

BLIND FAITH

Henry Fawcett (1833–1884), political economist, politician, campaigner for women's rights and Postmaster General, was born in Salisbury. He was pheasant shooting with his father in 1858 when he was accidentally shot by him and lost his sight completely. He told his father, 'Well, it shan't make any difference in my plans for life!' Although his career at the bar was cut short, he returned to Cambridge to become Professor of Political Economy, publishing his *Manual of Political Economy* in 1863.

He was MP for Brighton (1865–1874) and Hackney (1874–1884), and was Postmaster General (1880–1884) in Gladstone's government, responsible for introducing the parcel post, postal orders, and the sixpenny telegram to Britain.

He advanced the cause of blind people by advocating a Royal Commission on the blind in 1883, supported by Gladstone but not established until a year after his death. He was a supporter of equal rights and women's suffrage, encouraging his wife Millicent in the cause. She became leader of the National Union of Women's Suffrage Societies. There is a statue of Henry Fawcett in the Market Place, Salisbury.

SAVING OUR HERITAGE

Sir John Lubbock, 1st Baron Avebury (1834–1913) MP, banker, and scientific writer was responsible for the introduction of the 1871 Bank Holiday Bill which brought about the first secular holidays for workers. He helped protect Avebury and Silbury Hill from development by buying the monuments and surrounding lands in 1871 and pushed through the bill to preserve ancient monuments (1873). His other interests ranged from archaeology to zoology. He published *Prehistoric Times, as Illustrated by Ancient Remains*, and the *Manners and Customs of Modern Savages* (1865), where he introduced two new terms –Paleolithic and Neolithic (*see* Animals Tales).

HERE COME THE GIRLS ... SIX OF THE BEST

Down and Out in Oldham

Mary Higgs *née* Kingsland (1854–1937), poet, writer, social reformer and champion of women's rights, was born in Devizes. She was the first women to study natural sciences at Cambridge. She moved to Oldham with her congregational minister husband where she worked with the poor and the destitute. She disguised herself as a tramp to uncover conditions in local hostels, common lodging houses and workhouse wards, nearly thirty years before George Orwell published his *Down and Out in Paris and London*. Her books *Glimpses into the Abyss* (1906) and *Where Shall She Live? The Homelessness of the Woman Worker* (1910) drew on her experiences. She wrote poetry and a weekly column in two local Oldham newspapers and received an OBE for services to Oldham.

Saving the Children

Eglantyne Jebb (1876–1928) teacher and philanthropist, and her sister Dorothy Buxton (1881–1963), founded an emergency relief fund called Fight the Famine Council in 1919, which later became Save the Children Fund. Jebb came to St Peter's Boys School, Marlborough (now the Library), in 1899 for eighteen months but gave up work due to ill health. In her later travels, she took part in relief work among peasants in Macedonia after the Second Balkan War. In 1919, Jebb was arrested in Trafalgar Square for distributing leaflets featuring pictures of starving Austrian children. Although found guilty, she was fined only £5 and the Crown Prosecutor, Sir Archibald Bodkin, publicly pressed £5 into Jebb's hand. This became the first donation to the new charity, Save the Children Fund. The Princess Royal became president of Save the Children in 1970. There is a blue plaque to Jebb outside Marlborough Library.

Swindon's Suffragette

Edith Bessie New (1877–1951) was born at No. 24 North Street, Swindon. Her father was as a clerk at the GWR Works and her mother a music teacher. New taught at Queenstown Infant School (1899–1901) but left to teach in the east end of London. After hearing Emmeline Pankhurst speak in Trafalgar Square, she joined the Women's Social and Political Union (The Suffragettes). She was arrested in February 1907, along with two other women, after a demonstration in the House of Commons. She was sentenced to two weeks in Holloway Prison.

In June 1908, accompanied by Mary Leigh, she broke windows at No. 10 Downing Street and served two months in Holloway. In 1909, while campaigning in Scotland, she was arrested in Dundee, and sentenced to seven days in prisons where she and her fellow prisoners went on hunger strike. In 1911 she went back to teaching but continued to campaign for equal rights for women. In 1918 the Representation of the People Act was passed which allowed women over the age of thirty, who met a property qualification, to vote.

Making Working Life Better

Florence May Hancock (1893– 1974), trade union leader and second female President of the Trade Union Congress (TUC), was born at No. 14 Factory Lane in Chippenham and attended Westmead Junior School. She started work at the Nestle Condensed Milk Factory at fourteen, earning 5s 9d for a fifty-five-hour week. Prompted by the inhuman treatment of fellow workers, she campaigned all her life for better working conditions, especially for women and the low paid. On 14 January 1913 she led a successful two-week strike of the factory workers, the first strike at any factory in Chippenham, against 'tyrannical' management and low pay with no overtime. This began the Workers' Union in Wiltshire, and her campaigning as a full-time official from 1917 saw it grow so dramatically, that with 10,000 members by 1918, it was probably the second largest organisation in the county after the military.

From 1935 to 1958 she served continually on the General Council of the TUC, receiving the honour of Chairman in 1947 and President in 1948. Through this role she served on numerous Royal Commissions, including equal pay, work for disabled people, capital punishment and as an advisor for the International Labour Organisation. During the Second World War she was a special advisor to Minister of Labour, Ernest Bevin, advising on recruitment of women for war work, food production and rationing. She was granted a Damehood in 1951. She married widower, John Donovan, a colleague in the TGWU in 1963. She died while visiting her sister's home in King Alfred Street, Chippenham.

No Back Seat Driver

The Hon. Mrs Victor Bruce [*née* Mildred Petre] (1895–1990), motorist, aviatrix and businesswoman, lived at Priory Steps in Newtown, Bradford on Avon, from 1950 until her death. She pioneered mid-air refuelling in Britain and was an important figure in pre-war commercial aviation, establishing several freight and passenger airlines.

Marching Orders

Brigadier Dame Mary Railton (1906–1992), Director of the Women's Army Corps (1954–1957), is buried at St Mary's Church, Great Bedwyn, where her memorial reads: 'Gentle in manner, resolute in deed'.

BROTHER OF THE MORE FAMOUS

Arnold W. Lawrence (1900–1991), historian of ancient Greek sculpture and architecture, was the younger brother of T.E. Lawrence (of Arabia) and executor of his estate. He lived with friend Peggy Guido after his wife's death in 1986, in her house at No. 44 Long Street, Devizes, for the last few years of his life.

GREAT GUIDE

Sir Nikolaus Pevsner (1902–1983), architectural historian, is best known for *The Buildings of England* (1951–1974) one of the great achievements of twentieth-century art scholarship. Of the forty-six-book series he wrote thirty and collaborated on ten. He was born in Leipzig, moving to Britain to escape Nazism in 1933. He had a country cottage at Little Town, Broad Town, and was buried with his wife, Lola, who died in 1963, at St Peter's Church, Clyffe Pypard.

TWO WHEELS GOOD

Dr Alex Moulton (1920–2012), founder of Moulton Developments Ltd, inventor of the Moulton Bicycle and designer of the rubber suspension for the original Mini (launched 1959), lived at the seventeenth-century family home, The Hall in Bradford on Avon, from 1926 until his death. He went to Marlborough College where he astounded teachers with the steam car he designed and built, and the steel dodecahedron he constructed in the metalwork shop. He studied Mechanical Engineering at King's College Cambridge. He invented the first small-wheeled unisex bicycle with rigid frame, front and rear suspension and high-pressure tyres in 1962. It became popular with commuters and shoppers and could also be folded away for storage. The Moulton Bicycle Company is continued by his great-nephew, Shaun Moulton.

VACUUM MAN

Every thirty seconds a Dyson is sold in the UK. Malmesbury-based company Dyson reported record annual profit and turnover of more than £1bn (2011). King of the empire is Sir James Dyson, businessman, inventor and industrial designer. His invention of the dual cyclone bagless vacuum cleaner, 'The Dyson' DC01, became the fastest-selling vacuum cleaner ever made after its worldwide launch in 1993. It entered the permanent collections of the Design Museum of London, the Victoria & Albert Museum, the Design Museum of Zurich, and Paris's Centre Georges Pompidou. Other innovations include the Ballbarrow (1974), which won the Building Design Innovation Award in 1977; the Airblade hand dryer (2006), which is said to dry hands in ten seconds; and the Dyson Hot heater utilising ceramic stones (2010), which cannot burn you.

In 1993, Dyson built a combined factory and research and development establishment in Malmesbury. Production moved to Malaysia in 2002 but HQ and product design remain in the town, employing over 1,500 members of staff. The James Dyson Foundation was set up in 2002 'to promote the provision of facilities in the interest of social and community welfare' and 'to support a number of educational projects in the local community of Malmesbury'.

James Dyson's net worth is said to be £1.45 billion (2011), making him the richest person in the West of England.

BLUNT BROTHERS SCHOLARSHIP BOYS

The Spy

Anthony Frederick Blunt (1907–1983), art historian and spy, was a scholarship boy at Marlborough College, as were his two younger brothers Wilfrid and Christopher (*see* below). Their father, Arthur Blunt, was an Anglican minister who became chaplain to the British Embassy in Paris. Blunt won a mathematics scholarship to Trinity College Cambridge where he was invited to join the secret all-male Cambridge debating society, The Apostles. He was recruited by the KGB (intelligence service of the USSR) along with four others, into what became known as the Cambridge Five spy ring: Kim Philby, Donald Maclean, Guy Burgess and the fifth man, John Cairncross, who confessed to spying but not to being a member of the group.

Anthony Blunt became Professor of Art at the University of London, Director of the Courtauld Institute of Art and Surveyor of the King's pictures. He was stripped of his knighthood in 1979 and his honorary fellowship at Trinity College, which he had held since 1967.

The Coin Collector

Christopher Evelyn Blunt, OBE, FBA (1904–1987), scholar, numismatist and merchant banker, was the most influential figure in British numismatics during the twentieth century. He attended Marlborough College where he first became interested in coins and joined the Royal Numismatic Society at eighteen, having his first papers published ten years later. After he retired from banking he concentrated on collecting and studying coins; his special interest was in medieval British, and later in Anglo-Saxon, coins. He lived at Wilton House, Hungerford (1945–1952), before to moving to Ramsbury Hill in Ramsbury, near Marlborough, his home until his death. He was President of the British Numismatic Society from 1957 until 1961.

The Fitzwilliam Museum, Cambridge, acquired Christopher's collection of 3,663 Anglo- Saxon and later medieval coins and tokens in 1990, one of the most important private collections ever formed in this country.

The Calligrapher

Wilfrid Jasper Walter Blunt (1901–1987), art teacher and writer, attended Marlborough College from 1914 to 1920. He studied engraving at the Royal College of Art and trained as an opera singer in

Munich, joining Eton College in 1937 as a drawing master. His most acclaimed book was *The Art of Botanical Illustration* (1950) with botanist William T. Stearn, and *Sweet Roman Hand: Five Hundred Years of Italic Cursive Script* (1952). He was influential in the teaching of handwriting in British schools using the fifteenth-century Italian Cancellaresca Chancery Script. He retired from teaching in 1959 and became curator of the Watts Museum, Compton, until 1983.

Wilfrid Blunt

Sweet Roman Hand

five hundred years of Italic Cursive Script

IN OTHER WORDS

April FitzLyon (1920–1998), *née* Mead, musician, translator and biographer, was educated in France, attended St Mary's School in Calne and studied flute at the Guildhall School of Music. She lived in Russia with her Russian husband, Kyril Zinovieff (changed to FitzLyon), and together published the first translations of Chekhov *Short Stories* in Britain (1953). They later published a new translation of Tolstoy's *Anna Karenina*.

Translator of more than 200 children's books and more than 50 adult novels, mostly from German, Dutch and Scandinavian languages, including Thor Heyerdahl and Astrid Lindgren, Patricia Crampton has lived in Calne for over thirty years. She won the Marsh Award for Children's Literature in Translation (1999) for translating *The Final Journey* by Gudrun Pausewang. Mrs Crampton was one of the first non-Germans to hear about the atrocities that Pausewang described; her first job after Oxford University was as translator at the Nuremberg War Crimes Trials.

8

LITERARY WILTSHIRE

FIVE BEST-SELLING AUTHORS

The Railway Series books, including *Thomas the Tank Engine*, have sold over 200 million copies since publication of the first book (1945). Author Revd W.V. (Wilbert Vere) Awdry (1911–1997) lived at Journey's End, Box, between 1920 and 1928, and created the series for his son, Christopher, who was born in Devizes in 1940. Christopher took over the writing after his father's death, and also published the *Encyclopaedia of British Railway Companies* (1990). A blue plaque was unveiled on the house (now Lorne House B&B) in August 2012.

The Discworld fantasy novels of Wiltshire-resident Terry Pratchett have been translated into 21 languages, selling over 40 million books worldwide. Every new novel that Terry Pratchett writes sells in excess of 400,000 copies in paperback and 100,000 hardback in the UK alone. *Snuff* (2011) Discworld No. 39, became the third fastest-selling novel in the UK.

Salisbury resident, author Leslie Thomas has written more than 30 novels and has worldwide sales figures of over 14 million. His first book *The Virgin Soldiers* (1966) has sold over 7 million copies. His book *Almost Heaven: Tales from a Cathedral,* about Salisbury, was published in 2010.

Dick King-Smith (1922–2011), farmer, teacher and children's author, attended Marlborough College, afterwards working as an apprentice farmer in the Wylye valley. He wrote *The Sheep-Pig* (1983) which became the film *Babe* (1995). He set *The Crowstarver* (1998) on a Wiltshire farm at the outbreak of the Second World War. He wrote over 100 titles, translated into 12 languages and achieved sales of over 15 million.

Cressida Cowell, children's author and illustrator, attended Marlborough College (1982–1984). *How to Train Your Dragon* (2003), first in a series of ten books about Hiccup Horrrendous Haddock III, has sold more than three million copies. The film version (2010) grossed nearly $44 million in the opening weekend in the USA.

CRIME WRITING WORLD RECORD

John Creasey (1908–1973) creator of characters The Toff, The Baron, Inspector West and Gideon of the Yard, and founder of the Crime Writers' Association (CWA), still holds the record as the world's most prolific writer of crime fiction. He lived in New Hall, Bodenham, near Salisbury (1958–1973) and was buried at St Andrew's Church, Nunton. His house was converted into a hospital in 1979; in June 2007 a new ward was opened and named after the author.

Far from being a toff himself, he was the seventh of nine children born in Southfields, Surrey, where his father Joseph was a coachmaker. Creasey worked in a series of clerical and sales jobs, and due to childhood polio was rejected for service in the Second World War. His first published book *Seven Times Seven* (the tenth novel he had written) was published in 1932 by Melrose. He had received over 740 rejections from publishers up to the first acceptance. He wrote over 600 books, translated into over 28 languages. In one exceptional year he wrote 36 full-length books but his average was 12 to 15 a year.

Creasey also holds the record for most pseudonyms, writing under 28 names which distinguished different genres: Gordon Ashe, Norman Deane, Michael Halliday, Kyle Hunt, J.J. Marric, Anthony Morton and Jeremy York, to name but seven.

Many of his books were made into films and TV shows, including *Gideon's Way* (ITC, 1964–1967), with John Gregson in the title role. He was appointed MBE in 1946 for services in the National Savings Movement during the Second World War. He founded the All Party

Alliance in England which advocated government by the best men from all parties working together, and fought four by-elections.

A QUARTET OF LITERARY PRIESTS

William Lisle Bowles (1762–1850), clergyman and poet, was vicar of St Martin's Church in Bremhill from 1804 until shortly before his death in Salisbury. His volume *Fourteen Sonnets Written Chiefly on Picturesque Spots during a Journey* (1789) was very successful and admired by Coleridge. His major work was a ten-volume edition of the work of Alexander Pope with commentary (1806), causing much pubic controversy – not least with Byron (*see* entry below).

George Crabbe (1754–1832), poet and rector of St James' Church, Trowbridge (1814–1832), was ordained in 1782, and *The Village*, published in 1783, established his reputation as a poet. Jane Austen was a fan and named her heroine Fanny Price in *Mansfield Park* (1814) after a character in *The Parish Register* (1807). *The Borough* (1810) included the story of Peter Grimes, which inspired Benjamin Britten's opera of that name. His final published work *Tales of the Hall* was sold to a publisher in 1819 for £3,000 (equivalent to £125,800 in 2005). There is a memorial tablet to Crabbe on the north wall of the chancel of St James', Trowbridge.

George Herbert (1593–1633), poet, hymn writer and MP for Montgomery (1624–1625), was rector of Fugglestone-with-Bemerton, near Salisbury from 1630 until 1633. He is best known as one of the Metaphysical Poets, along with John Donne and Andrew Marvell. *The Temple: Sacred Poems and Private Ejaculations* (1633), published posthumously, went through eight editions by 1690. He composed the words of hymns 'Let all the world in every corner sing' and 'The God of Love my Shepherd Is'. He loved Evensong at

Salisbury Cathedral, calling it 'Heaven upon earth', and cared deeply for his parishioners, paying for the restoration of the church in 1630. He died of tuberculosis and was buried near the altar in St Andrew's Church, Bemerton. There is a memorial window to Herbert in St George's Chapel, Westminster Abbey.

Francis Kilvert (1840–1879), clergyman and diarist, was born at The Rectory, Hardenhuish Lane, Chippenham, but the family moved to the new rectory near Langley Common in 1857. Kilvert became curate to his father at Langley Burrell. He was also curate in Clyro, Radnorshire and vicar at St Harmon, Radnorshire, and at Brewardine, Herefordshire. He wrote his diaries from 1870 until his last entry on 23 September 1879, the day before he died from peritonitis.

He completed twenty-nine notebooks but his widow destroyed seven. Twenty-two remained within his family until his nephew, Percival Smith, saw their potential and took them to publisher Jonathan Cape. The manuscript was edited by poet and author, William Plomer, and published in three volumes (1938–1940) to critical acclaim. Sadly, after the originals were returned to the family, a niece destroyed all but three in a clear out of her home. One volume was donated to Durham University and two bought by the National Library of Wales.

BYRON CONNECTIONS

Famously described by Lady Caroline Lamb as 'Mad, bad, and dangerous to know', poet Lord George Gordon Byron (1788–1824) was a regular visitor to Bowood House, Calne. The Albanian costume which Byron wore in the famous portrait of him by Thomas Phillips (1813), now in the National Portrait Gallery, is displayed at Bowood.

In 1817, Ireland's national poet Thomas Moore (1779–1852) moved from Dublin with his family to Sloperton Cottage, Westbrook, near Bromham. He frequently visited his friend and patron, Lord Henry Petty-Fitzmaurice, the 3rd Marquess of Lansdowne, 4th Earl of Kerry at Bowood House. He used the library and was a popular guest at social gatherings, where he enjoyed the company of other visitors such as Byron and Shelley. Moore would sing, dance and recite poetry. 'Sung in the evening and made Lady Louisa's governess (as I heard afterwards) cry most profusely.' He wrote his *Notices of the Life of Lord Byron* in 1835. His songs and poems, including 'A Minstrel Boy', 'The Last Rose of Summer' and 'Believe Me, if all Those Endearing Young Charms', are still popular today. Moore was buried at St Nicholas Church, Bromham. Words by Byron are inscribed on his memorial Celtic cross: 'The poet of all circles and the idol of his own'.

INSPIRED BY WILTSHIRE

Arthur C. Clarke (1917–2008), science fiction writer, used his experiences as a radar operator and instructor at RAF Yatesbury during the Second World War in his book *Glide Path* (1963). He was in charge of the first radar 'talk-down' equipment, the Ground Controlled Approach, during its experimental trials.

Much of *Martin Chuzzlewit* (1844) by Charles Dickens was set in Salisbury. 'Mr Pinch had a shrewd notion that Salisbury was a very desperate sort of place; an exceeding wild and dissipated city ... its being market-day, and the thoroughfares about the market-place being filled with carts, horses, donkeys, baskets, waggons, garden-stuff, meat, tripe, pies, poultry and huckster's wares of every opposite description and possible variety of character.'

Betsey Trotwood in *David Copperfield* (1850) is based on Mary Pearson Strong (1768–1851), who was born in Erlestoke and moved to Broadstairs with her parents. She had an aversion to donkeys which she chased away from the house, obviously something Dickens drew upon for his character from his visits to the family.

The Waggon and Horses Inn at Beckhampton is the setting for the Bagman's story in *The Pickwick Papers* (1837). 'It was a strange old place, built of a kind of shingle, inlaid, as it were, with cross-beams, with gabled-topped windows projecting completely over the pathway, and a low door with a dark porch, and a couple of steep steps leading down into the house.'

Jasper Fforde lived in Marlborough for twelve years and set his series of novels featuring his literary detective Thursday Next in a parallel Swindon. The first one, *The Eyre Affair* (2001), was rejected seventy-six times. He was listed at number eight in David Baldacci's 'Ten Greatest Fictional Detectives' published in the *Daily Mail* 2011.

Ghost Knight (2012) by children's author Cornelia Funke, is set in and around Salisbury Cathedral, inspired by the story of William Longespée and his wife Ela, the first female High Sheriff of Wiltshire and founder of Lacock Abbey.

Robert Goddard explains why he chose Swindon as a setting in his Harry Barnett thrillers, *Out of the Blue*, *Into the Sun* and *Past Caring*: 'I wanted somewhere resolutely unglamorous for Harry Barnett to come from and because I knew the town had an interesting history I could use as background colour. Also because a WHSmith HQ staff member based in Swindon once said to me that it was a pity no thrillers were ever set there.' *Caught in the Light* (1998) is set partly in Lacock, and *Sight Unseen* (2005) in Avebury. The title *In Pale Battalions* (1986) is taken from a line by Charles Hamilton Sorley (*see* entry below).

Mark Haddon set his Whitbread Novel of the Year 2003, *The Curious Incident of the Dog in the Night-time*, in Swindon.

Salisbury became Melchester in Thomas Hardy's novels. The King's House, in The Close (home to the Salisbury and South Wiltshire Museum), was the setting for the teacher training college that Sue Bridehead attended in *Jude the Obscure* (1895).

Man Booker Prize-winner *Wolf Hall* (2009) by Hilary Mantel recreates the life of Thomas Cromwell and his relationship with Henry VIII at court during his divorce from Katharine of Aragon and plans for wife number two, Anne Boleyn. The book ends as the arrival of Jane Seymour of Wolf Hall (also Wulfhall), the Seymour family seat in the parish of Great Bedwyn, now Burbage. Her father was warden of Savernake Forest. The sequel *Bring up the Bodies* (2012) continues the story of the destruction of Anne Boleyn and the rise of Jane Seymour.

Sarum (1987) the first book by Salisbury-born historical novelist Edward Rutherfurd (Francis Edward Wintle), is set in Stonehenge and Salisbury and tells the story of five families from the Ice Age to the present day. It is dedicated 'to those who built and to those who are now trying to save Salisbury Spire'. The book became an instant international bestseller, remaining twenty-three weeks on the *New York Times* Bestseller List. In 2005, the City of Salisbury commemorated Rutherfurd's contribution to the city by naming a street leading off the Market Place, Rutherfurd Walk.

Wiltshire's forgotten war poet, Charles Hamilton Sorley (1895–1915) was educated at Marlborough College (1908–1913) and had poems published in the school magazine *The Marlburian*. He spent seven months in Germany after leaving school and enlisted in the 7th Battalion Suffolk Regiment in 1914. He arrived in France on 30 May 1915, where he served near Ploegsteert. He was promoted to Captain in August and died at the Battle of Loos, 13 October 1915, from a shot in the head by a sniper. *Sonnet XXXIV*, probably the last poem he wrote, was found in his kit bag after his death. It begins:

'When you see millions of the mouthless dead
Across your dreams in pale battalions go...'

His book, *Marlborough and Other Poems*, was published posthumously in 1916.

The Suspicions of Mr Whicher (2008) by Kate Summerscale tells the story of the detective who tried to solve the notorious Road Hill House (now Langham House, Rode) Murder which took place on 30 June 1860. Three-year-old Saville Kent's dead body was found at his home stuffed down the outside privy and his sixteen-year-old half-sister, Constance, later confessed to the crime.

Edward Thomas (1878–1917), poet, wrote *Lob* about the beauty of Wiltshire and its place names 'Manningfords – Abbots, Bohun and Bruce,' while searching for an old man he had once met. He was stationed at Codford Camp in January 1917 before going out to France where he was killed by a shell on 9 April, the first day of the Battle of Arras.

Anthony Trollope (1815–1882) managed to combine his career in the Postal Service, where he rose to the rank of senior civil servant, with writing. In May 1852, his work brought him to Salisbury. In *An Autobiography*, he recalled wandering around the city and cathedral and standing 'for an hour on the little bridge in Salisbury, and had made out to my own satisfaction the spot on which Hiram's hospital should stand'. This became the setting for *The Warden*, the first in his series of novels set in imaginary Barchester.

BORN IN WILTSHIRE

International bestseller *Sperm War – Infidelity, Sexual Conflict and Other Bedroom Battles* (1996) and other books by Robin Baker, evolutionary biologist, writer, and broadcaster, have been translated into twenty-eight different languages. Born in Wiltshire, he was brought up in Manningford Bruce and attended Marlborough Grammar School. He was Reader in Zoology in the School of Biological Sciences at the University of Manchester (1980–1996).

Overlooked and underrated Nigel Balchin (1908–1970), novelist, screenwriter and industrial psychologist, was born in The Butts, Potterne, and attended Dauntsey's School, West Lavington (1919–1927). He studied Natural Sciences at Cambridge and joined the National Institute for Industrial Psychology, becoming a consultant to J.S. Rowntree & Son in York. He is credited with designing the black and white box for Black Magic, and in helping to develop Aero. Did he put the bubbles into the chocolate bar? During the war he was scientific advisor to the Army Council which influenced his writing. He adapted his own work *The Small Back Room* (1943) and *Mine Own Executioner* (1945) for the screen, and his screenplay of Ewen Montagu's book *The Man Who Never Was* won him a BAFTA (1956). He wrote the screenplay for *The Singer not the Song* (1961) which starred Dirk Bogarde, adapted from a novel by Audrey Erskine Lindop.

The Wiltshire Heritage Museum, Library and Gallery were set up and are administered by the Wiltshire Archaeological & Natural History Society (WANHS). It was founded in Devizes in 1853, after the acquisition of the John Britton library of topographical and antiquarian books and manuscripts by a group of local gentlemen. John Britton (1771–1875), antiquary and topographer, born in Kington St Michael, is best known for T*he Beauties of England and Wales* (1801) and *The Beauties of Wiltshire* (1825).

Author and armaments manufacturer, John Meade Falkner (1858 –1932), best known for *Moonfleet* (1898), was born in Manningford Bruce and educated at Marlborough College and Hertford College, Oxford. He became tutor to the sons of Andrew Noble, an armaments manufacturer, eventually joining Sir W.G. Armstrong & Co. as secretary to the board and then as overseas negotiator. He also wrote guidebooks on Oxford and Berkshire, *The Lost Stradivarius* (1895) and *The Nebuly Coat* (1903). He was awarded a papal medal for his work on Vatican manuscripts. His wealth at his death was £215,524.7s.1d (equivalent to over £7 million in 2005).

The 'female Pepys', Celia Fiennes (1662–1741), traveller and diarist, was born in Newton Tony. Daughter of Colonel Nathaniel Fiennes, a Parliamentarian Officer, she began her travels to regain her health 'by variety and change of aire and exercise' aged twenty-two, and went on to visit every county in England. Her journal *Through England on a Side Saddle in the Time of William and Mary*, written for family and friends from 1695 onwards, was first published in 1888.

Richard Jefferies (1848–1887), naturalist and writer, was born on the family farm at Coate, Chiseldon. He was a reporter on the *North Wilts Herald* and became famous for a 4,000 word letter to *The Times*, on the plight of the Wiltshire agricultural labourer. Works include *The Gamekeeper at Home* (1878), *The Amateur Poacher* (1879), *Hodge and his Masters* (1880) and *Bevis: the Story of a Boy* (1882).

Arthur George Street, aka 'AG' Street, writer, farmer and broadcaster, was born at Ditchampton Farm in Wilton, and went to Dauntsey's School, leaving at fifteen to join his father working on the farm. He was the author of twenty-five books including *Farmer's Glory* (1932) and wrote regularly for *Farmers' Weekly*. He lived at Mill Farm, South Newton, from 1950 until his death.

John Whiting (1917–1963) actor and playwright, famous for *Penny for a Song* (1951) and *The Devils* (1960) was born in Salisbury.

Alfred Owen Williams (1877–1930), 'Hammerman Poet' and writer on rural and industrial life, was born in Cambria Cottage, The Hook, South Marston, in Swindon. He and his wife later built their own house, Ranikhet, nearby. He started work on a farm at the age of eight and after three years went to work at the Great Western Railway Works until 1914, when he left due to ill health. He wrote *Life in a Railway Factory* (1915) 'the only good book on factory life,' he said, 'that we have in England written by a working man'. His vivid account is a reminder of a past world: 'Then the riveters knocked down the head of the rivet with long-nosed hammers, striking alternately in rapid succession and making the neighbourhood resound with the blows.'

He was a self-taught man, teaching himself Latin and Greek and enrolling in a correspondence course in English Literature at Ruskin Hall, Oxford. He volunteered for army service in 1916 and served in India, where taught himself Sanskrit. He wrote about Wiltshire folk life in *A Wiltshire Village* (1912), *Villages of the White Horse* (1913) and *Round about the Upper Thames* (1922).

GODOLPHIN GIRL POWER

Dorothy L. Sayers, (1893–1957), scholar, writer and creator of detective Lord Peter Wimsey, who first appeared in *Whose Body?* (1923); Jilly Cooper, aka queen of the bonkbuster, author of *Rivals, Riders* and *Polo*, and Minette Walters, aka queen of the psychological thriller, author of *The Scold's Bridle*, *The Sculptress* and *The Ice House*, all attended Godolphin School in Salisbury.

WILTSHIRE RESIDENTS

The Heretick, Marlborough College's student magazine, was founded in 1924 by John Betjeman who attended the college in 1920 to 1925. Contributors included Louis MacNeice and Anthony Blunt, the art historian and spy. Betjeman's time at Marlborough was not happy and is described in his blank verse autobiographical poem *Summoned by Bells* (1960). He was knighted in 1969 and became Poet Laureate in 1972. His daughter, author and journalist Candida Lycett-Green, lived at Blackland, Calne, where she held a party for her father's seventieth birthday in 1976.

Mavis Cheek, author of *Amenable Women*, *Mrs Fytton's Country Life* and *Janice Gentle Gets Sexy*, lives in Aldbourne.

Lauren Child, children's author and illustrator, creator of *Charlie and Lola* and *Clarice Bean*, grew up in Marlborough where she attended St John's School and Marlborough College.

Samuel Taylor Coleridge (1772–1834), poet and critic, was sent to stay with Dr John Morgan and his family at Bentley House on Church Street, Calne, in March 1815, to write but mainly to keep him out of trouble – i.e. to get him off drugs. Coleridge completed his *Biographia Literaria* on 29 July 1815, fuelled, no doubt, by the laudanum he managed to get from High Street druggist, Thomas Bishop. His new play *Remorse* was performed at the Assembly Rooms in Calne before his return to London in March 1816 due to illness.

Denis Constanduros (1910–1978), scriptwriter, artist and author, lived at Coombe Bissett near Salisbury from 1938. He co-wrote the radio serial *At the Linscombes* (1948–1962), a story of country folk in the imaginary village of Dimstock in the Wyle valley. He adapted many books for TV including *Love and Mr Lewshiam* (1959), *The Railway Children* (1968), *Emma* (1972) and *Sense and Sensibility* (1981). The Salisbury and District Cricket Club still awards the Denis Constanduros Trophy for the Youth League Under-16 Division 1.

Marian Evans (1819–1880), aka George Eliot the novelist, visited Wiltshire on a number of occasions. In 1834, she stayed at Sandcliffe House, Northgate Street, Devizes, the home of Dr Robert Brabant, who was the physician to Irish poet Thomas Moore (*see* above) who lived near Bromham. She is said to have modelled her character Edward Casaubon in *Middlemarch* on Dr Brabant. On another visit in 1874 she stayed at The Bear Hotel.

Henry Fielding (1707–1754), novelist, regularly visited his grandmother in St Martin's Church Street, near St Anne's Gate in the Cathedral Close, eventually marrying a local girl who lived at No. 14, The Close. He stayed at Milford Manor about the time he was writing *Tom Jones*. A pane of glass from a window of the summerhouse, engraved by him with the inscription 'Dear Clarissa – Puellarum omnium formissima, She's the fairest where thousands are fair', is stored at Salisbury and South Wiltshire Museum.

Ian Fleming (1908–1964), former naval intelligence officer, author and creator of James Bond, had a house in Sevenhampton near Highworth and is buried at the local church of St James.

Geoffrey Grigson (1905–1985), poet, critic and writer, lived at Broad Town Farm House for nearly thirty years until his death. He founded the magazine *New Verse* in 1933, and his first book of poetry was *Several Observations* (1939). His *Collected Poems* appeared in 1963. He is buried in Christ Church, Broad Town – his stone is inscribed, 'The petals of my particular rose have fallen'.

His third wife, cookery writer Jane Grigson (1928–1990), lived at Broad Town Farm House for thirty-five years. From 1968 until a week before her death, Jane wrote for the *Observer Magazine*, having been recommended by Elizabeth David. In spite of being terminally ill, she spoke and raised funds to fight off threats from developers at nearby Avebury. She was buried alongside her husband. She bequeathed her collection of cookery books to the Guildhall Library in the City of London.

Daughter, Sophie Grigson, cookery writer and chef, was born in Swindon. She first appeared on TV in 1993 in her own series *Grow Your Own Greens* in 1993. She won the Guild of Food Writers Cookery Journalist Award in 2001.

Hammond Innes (1913–1998), thriller writer, lived in Aldbourne (1946–1947) where he wrote *The Lonely Skier*, *Killer Mine* and *Maddon's Rock*.

John Lockwood Kipling (1837–1911), father of Rudyard Kipling and illustrator of some of his son's early books, such as *The Jungle Book* (1894–1895), retired to The Gables, Hindon Lane in Tisbury. He and his wife, Alice, were buried behind the chancel of St John the Baptist Church, Tisbury. Rudyard rented Arundell House near to his parents from time to time, and it was here that he wrote *Kim* (1901).

Derrick Somerset Macnutt (1902–1971), known as Ximenes, cryptic crossword compiler for the *Observer*, attended Marlborough College. Particular fans were P.G. Wodehouse, Leonard Bernstein and Stephen Sondheim. Four hundred solvers were present at the celebration party in 1968 for Crossword No. 1,000.

Philip Massinger (1583–1640), playwright, was born near Salisbury and baptised at St Thomas's Church, Salisbury. Sixteen of his own plays survive, but he also collaborated with Thomas Dekker and John Fletcher who took over as chief playwright to the King after Shakespeare's death in 1616. A playwright could earn £6 for a play in the 1590s, and £20 by 1610s (equivalent to £2,000 in 2005).

Adrian Mitchell (1932– 2008), poet and playwright, went to Greenways Preparatory School, Codford, and Dauntsey's School.

Bel Mooney, journalist and novelist, attended Trowbridge Girls' High School between 1960 and 1966, where she was in the winning team of the Inter-schools Debating Festival, 1965. She currently writes an advice column for the *Daily Mail*.

Sir Henry Newbolt (1862–1938), poet and writer, famous for *Drake's Drum* and *Vitaï Lampada (Torch of Life)* with its refrain 'Play up, play up, and play the game', lived at Netherhampton House (1907–1934), former home of the Gauntlet pipe-maker family of Amesbury. He was head of the War Propaganda Bureau and controller of communications during the First World War.

R.J. Yeatman (1897–1968), co-author of *1066 and All That* (1930) with W.C. Sellar (whom he met at Oxford) attended Marlborough College.

THREE LITERARY HOTSPOTS

Safe House

Poet and writer, Siegfried Sassoon (1886–1967) was commissioned in the Royal Welch Fusiliers and posted to France in 1915 and awarded the MC for bravery. He bought Heytesbury House near Warminster in 1933 for £20,000 and lived there until his death. He entertained guests such as William Walton, Hilaire Belloc, T.E. Lawrence and Ottoline Morrell. At the beginning of the Second World War he billeted evacuees, and American troops camped in his grounds. Later, Sassoon looked after 200 books and manuscripts for his friend Sydney Cockerell, Director of the Fitzwilliam Museum.

Entertaining at Home

Socialite, aesthete and artist (and one-time lover of Siegfried Sassoon) Stephen Tennant (1906–1986) lived at the family home Wilsford Manor near Amesbury all his life. He was said to be the inspiration for Sebastian Flyte in Evelyn Waugh's *Brideshead Revisited* (1945) and Cedric Hampton in Nancy Mitford's *Love in a Cold Climate* (1949). During the war, Wilsford Manor was taken over by the Red Cross and afterwards Tennant redesigned the grounds into an English Côte d'Azur, with twenty-two tons of sand, palm trees and tropical birds, and lizards loose in the grounds. He pretty much retired to bed for the next seventeen years in what his biographer Philip Hoare called 'decorative reclusion', where he entertained visitors such as Christopher Isherwood, Truman Capote and David Hockney. In later years, Tennant would go shopping locally wearing tight pink shorts or a tablecloth as a skirt. His ashes are interred at St Michael's, Wilsford-cum-Lake.

Bloomsbury Love Nest

Dora loved Lytton who loved Ralph who loved Lytton but married Dora. And they all set up home in the Grade II listed Ham Spray House, Ham, near Marlborough, which Lytton and Ralph bought for £2,300 in 1924 (for sale in 2008 for £2.75 million).

Giles Lytton Strachey (1880–1932), writer and biographer, including *Eminent Victorians*, died at Ham Spray House.

Dora Carrington (1893–1932), artist, who was married to Ralph Partridge, committed suicide at Ham Spray House soon after her friend Lytton Strachey died. Her ashes were buried under the laurels in the garden of the house.

Ralph Partridge (1894–1960), soldier and writer, married Dora Carrington and then Frances Marshall, and continued to live in Ham Spray House until his death.

A friend once described Ham Spray House as 'a centre of loving hospitality and enlightenment and the greatest civilized taste in all things'.

9

WILTSHIRE'S NOBEL LAUREATE

William Gerald Golding (1911–1993), Nobel Prize-winning author, was born in Cornwall but lived in the family home on The Green in Marlborough until a young man. He attended Marlborough Grammar School where his father, Alec, was senior assistant master. He studied natural science at Brasenose College, Oxford, but after two years transferred his course to study English Literature. Shortly after marrying Ann Brookfield he moved back to Wiltshire to join the staff of Bishop Wordsworth's School, Salisbury, where he taught English and Greek literature in translation.

WARTIME

He joined the Royal Navy in 1940 as an ordinary seaman but became an officer, being sent to work at a secret research centre under Churchill's scientific adviser, Professor Lindemann. He was given command of a small rocket-launching craft. He was involved in the chase and the sinking of the *Bismarck*, and took part in the D-Day assault on Fortress Europe in 1944.

TEACHING

He returned to Bishop Wordsworth's School in 1945 and began writing seriously. His nickname at school was 'Scruff' because of his scruffy beard, hair and clothes. Old Boys of the school, who were taught by Golding, remember that he wrote books during lessons. Some helped to count the words on the pages of his latest manuscript for the publishers. Golding left teaching in 1961 to write full time.

REJECTION

The original title of *Lord of the Flies* was *Strangers from Within*. Twenty-one publishers had rejected it before it reached Faber and Faber – it was rejected again. Their professional reader scribbled comments that it was absurd, dull and pointless. Luckily, Charles Monteith, an eagle-eyed new junior sub-editor, spotted it, read it and liked it.

PUBLICATION

Faber and Faber paid Golding an advance of £60 for the book and it was published on 17 September 1954. It became his most successful book, selling over 10 million copies and available now in more than 35 languages.

REVIEWS AT THE TIME

'I fell under the terrible spell of this book and so will many others' Pat Murphy, *Daily Mail*
'This beautiful and desperate book, something quite out of the ordinary' Stevie Smith, the *Observer*
'Not only a splendid novel but morally and theologically impeccable' T.S. Eliot
'Readable and bloodcurdling' John Betjeman
'Beautifully written, tragic and provocative' E.M. Forster

MEMORIAL SERVICE

Golding died on 19 June 1993 and was buried under a huge yew tree in Holy Trinity churchyard, Bowerchalke. His wife, Ann, died in 1995 and is buried beside him. At his memorial service in Salisbury

Cathedral on 20 November 1993, a boy from Bishop Wordsworth's School read the account of Simon's death from *Lord of the Flies* and Poet Laureate, Ted Hughes, read passages from *The Inheritors*. Music played included 'Prologue and Epilogue' from *Serenade for Tenor Horn and Strings* by Benjamin Britten and Raymond Leppard's *Kyrie Eleison* from the film score of *Lord of the Flies*.

GOLDING'S WILTSHIRE HOMES

No. 29, The Green, Marlborough
No. 21, Bourne Avenue, Salisbury
Flat 2, St Mark's House, Salisbury
Ebble Thatch, Bowerchalke, near Salisbury.

GOLDING'S NOVELS

Lord of the Flies, 1954
The Inheritors, 1955
Pincher Martin, 1956
Free Fall, 1959
The Spire, 1964
The Pyramid, 1967
The Scorpion God, 1971
Darkness Visible, 1979
Rites of Passage, 1980
The Paper Men, 1984
Close Quarters, 1987
Fire Down Below, 1989
The Double Tongue, 1995

AWARDS AND PRIZES

Fellow of the Royal Society of Literature, 1955
CBE, 1966
Honorary Doctorate University of Sussex, 1968
Honorary Doctorate University of Kent, 1974
Booker-McConnell Prize, 1980 (*Rites of Passage*)
Nobel Prize For Literature, 1983
Honorary Doctorates University of Oxford and The Sorbonne (Paris), 1983
Companion of Literature, 1984

Honorary Doctorate University of Bristol, 1984
Knighthood, 1988
Honorary Doctorate University of Oviedo (Spain) 1992

LORD OF THE FLIES – THREE FILM VERSIONS

The 1963 Version
Black and white, directed by Peter Brooks (92 mins)
Filmed: 17 April 1961 – August 1961
Budget: $250,000 (estimated)

Cast:

Ralph	James Aubrey
Jack	Tom Chapin
Piggy	Hugh Edwards
Roger	Roger Elwin
Simon	Tom Gaman

Film Locations:
Chattanooga, Tennessee, Frenchman's Cove, Port Antonio, Jamaica, Puerto Rica, Jamaica

Trivia:
Eleven-year-old Hugh Edwards, who played Piggy in the film, landed his role by writing a letter to the director which read, 'Dear Sir, I am fat and wear spectacles.'
It was one of the first films to be shot using a hand-held camera.

The 1975 Alkitrang Dugo
Filipino version of the film, with a mixed cast of boys and girls and directed by Lupito Aquino-Kashiwahara.

The 1990 Version
Filmed in colour, directed by Harry Hook (90 mins).

Cast:

Ralph	Balthazar Getty
Jack	Chris Furrh
Piggy	Danuel Pipoly
Roger	Gary Rule
Simon	James Badge Dale

Film Locations:
Hamuka Coast, Hawaii, Los Angeles County Arboretum & Botanic Gardens, Port Antonio, Jamaica

DRAMATISATIONS

In 1955 there was an attempt at a stage version of *Lord of the Flies* by American playwright Carolyn Green. It was called *This Wonderful Island*, but Golding refused to allow it or any other dramatisation for the next thirty years.

Lord of the Flies was eventually adapted for the stage by the novelist Nigel Williams and first produced by the Royal Shakespeare Company at Stratford upon Avon in 1995.

A Sea Trilogy: Rites of Passage, *Close Quarters* and *Fire Down Below* were dramatised in a three-part BBC film series (2005) entitled *To the Ends of the Earth*, starring Benedict Cumberbatch, Sam Neill, Victoria Hamilton and Jared Harris.

The premiere of Roger Spottiswoode's adaptation of Golding's *The Spire* (director Gareth Machin) took place at the Salisbury Playhouse, 1 November 2012.

10

MUSICAL WILTSHIRE

EARLY MUSIC STARS

Andrew Markes of Salisbury, whose father was a fiddle maker, was the best lutenist in England in his time during the latter end of Queen Elizabeth I's reign (1558–1603) and King James's reign (1567–1625).

Musician to Oliver Cromwell and then Charles II, Davys Mell was born in Wilton and died in 1662. Said to be the best violinist of any Englishman in England he was also a renowned clock and watchmaker.

Humphrey Madge of Salisbury, instrumentalist, was appointed on 10 July 1660 to King Charles II as cornettist and flutist at £40 12s 8d p.a. In addition he took over as court violinist and violist at £40 p.a., with occasional livery allowances of £16 2s 6d for each of these positions. When he attended at Hampton Court in the summer of 1662, he received daily expenses of 5s. Pepys mentions in his diary hearing Madge on a number of occasions – although not always at his best: '10 March 1660, went … to my office, whither also Mr. Madge comes half foxed (intoxicated) and played the fool upon the violin that made me weary'.

Henry Lawes, singer and composer who wrote music for Milton's masque *Comus*, and brother, William Lawes, instrumentalist and composer, were born in Dinton near Wilton and baptised in Salisbury. They both held positions at Charles I's court. William was appointed to the King's Musick as one of the 'lutes and voices', and Henry became a member of the Chapel Royal, as well as later composing for Charles II.

Michael Wise, composer, organist and master of choristers at Salisbury Cathedral in 1668 was born in Wiltshire, probably in Salisbury.

In spite of his slightly tarnished reputation, including a fine of 10s for absenteeism, he was appointed to the post of almoner (master of the choristers) of St Paul's Cathedral on 27 January 1687. He died 24 August 1687 in Salisbury, following a violent quarrel with his wife. It was reported that 'he was knock'd on the head & killed downright by the Night–watch (constables) at Salisbury for giving stubborne and refractory language to them, on S. Bartholomews day [24 August] at night.' He was buried at St Thomas's Church, Salisbury.

... AND MORE RECENT STARS

World-famous Australian opera singer, Dame Nellie Melba, who gave her name to Peach Melba and Melba Toast, appeared at the Garrison Theatre, Tidworth, on 11 June 1926. This was her final performance in this country before retiring, after having made her farewell appearance three days before at Covent Garden, London, in the presence of King George V and Queen Mary.

Canada's Yodelling Cowboy, Alberta Slim, pioneer of country music in Canada, was born Eric Edwards in Wilsford. He emigrated to Canada with his family in 1920 where he became an early radio star, playing guitar and singing, and adopting the technique of echo yodelling. He recorded over 100 of his own songs with R.C.A. Victor, many about Canadian heroes and life on the prairies. He also formed his own travelling circus which included Susie, a harmonica-playing elephant, singing dogs, a blue donkey and his own horse called Kitten which told fortunes. He was still performing at the age of ninety-three.

'The Royal Opera House Covent Garden has paid another tribute to Arthur Carron, the Swindon tenor, formerly principal tenor at the Metropolitan Opera House, New York and Teatro Colon, Buenos Aires. He has accepted an invitation to sing the role of Herod in Oscar Wilde's Salome in which occurs the famous "Dance of the Seven Veils" ... Recently Mr Carron declined an invitation to tour Australia in connection with the festivities of the Commonwealth Jubilee.' (*The Wiltshire Herald & Advertiser*, 12 January 1951)

In a radio broadcast to America in April 1958, Yehudi Menhuin played a violin made from one of Winston Churchill's cigar boxes. This was the work of self-taught violin maker William Robinson of Plumstead (1880–1960). He was a former master saddler from Avebury who spent his childhood converting empty boxes into rustic violins. The wife of Prime Minister Anthony Eden, who admired

Robinson's work and knew of his wish to make one, obtained a cigar box for him. In his career up to 1953 he made 400 violins, 40 violas and 16 cellos.

Rosemary Squires, 'Britain's Answer to Doris Day', was born in 1928 in Salisbury where she was brought up. Her first broadcast was at the age of twelve and her first BBC Radio series was in 1949. She sang the advertising jingle 'Now hands that do dishes can feel soft as your face with mild green Fairy Liquid' in the 1960s, which continued to be used for forty years. She has performed all over the world alongside stars such as Danny Kaye, Sammy Davis Jnr and Cliff Richards. She received an MBE in 2004 for services to music and charity. In 2012 she toured with her show, *Those Were the Days – Sixty Years of Song*.

Buddy Holly and the Crickets performed a matinée and two evening shows at the Gaumont Theatre, Salisbury, on 22 March 1958. They played 'That'll be The Day', 'Peggy Sue', 'Oh Boy', 'Maybe Baby' and 'Everyday'. Buddy, the Crickets, their manager and recording engineer, Norman Petty, his wife, Vi, and road manager, Wally Stewart, all stayed at The Old George Hotel on the High Street. Between shows, Buddy went sightseeing, visiting the new American Soda-Bar which had just opened in Woolworths.

The Everly Brothers played at the Gaumont Salisbury with Bo Diddley, Little Richard and The Rolling Stones on 27 October 1963.

The Rolling Stones moved up the bill when they appeared a month later at McIlroys Ballroom on Regent Street, Swindon, 21 November 1963, supported by Frankie Roy and the Soundcasters. *Swindon Evening Advertiser* reviewed the performance, giving prominence to lead guitarist Brian Jones: 'His command of the style is authoritative, and he managed to achieve a mellow, amplified sound where most West Country "rock" groups only muster a harsh twang.'

The Kinks played at the Neeld Hall, Chippenham, on 7 September 1964. They had to drop their instruments and flee the stage when a mass of excited and hysterical fans surged forward and leaped onto the stage during 'You Really Got Me'.

ABBA, who sold more than 100 million records, with nine UK number one hits including 'Waterloo', 'Dancing Queen' and 'Mamma Mia', had the headquarters of their Official Fan Club in Sheep Street, Highworth, Swindon.

Devizes-born Simon May, musician and composer, attended Dauntsey's School. He composed theme tunes to *Eastenders* and *Howard's Way* as well as *Castaway*, *City Hospital*, *Dealing with Dickinson*, *Eldorado*, *Food & Drink* and *Pet Rescue*, and film music for *The Dawning* (1988) and 'I'm in Love' sung by Ruby Turner in *The Jewel of the Nile* (1985). He co-wrote the musical *Smike* and has written ten UK Top 20 hits, with record sales in excess of five million. He is Patron of the Devizes Junior Eisteddfod and Patron of the Swindon 105.5 Community Radio Station.

THE BEATLES IN WILTSHIRE

The Beatles played at McIlroys Ballroom (aka Macs) on Regent Street, Swindon, on 17 July 1962. Pete Best was drummer. In spite of an advertisement for the event in the *Swindon Advertiser*: 'TONIGHT, the Fabulous Beat Group from Liverpool' and 'The Most Popular group in the North' only 360 people turned up, particularly disappointing for the band as the venue's capacity was over 1,500. The event had been promoted by Jaybee Clubs organisation and the Beatles were paid the princely sum of £27 10s for the night.

By the time the Beatles came to Salisbury they had released their first single 'Love Me Do', brought out on 5 October 1962, which reached number 17 in the charts – it was a number one in the US in 1964.

15 June 1963, the Beatles performed at the City Hall on Fisherton Street, Salisbury. This concert was booked in April 1963 by Brian Epstein and promoted by Jaybee Clubs. Epstein agreed a fee of £300 for the show but afterwards grew concerned about the group's safety at the venue. Epstein offered Jaybee £200 to cancel the booking, but was turned down. Luckily, 1,500 people watched The Beatles play that night.

2–6 May 1965, the Beatles came to Salisbury Plain to film *Help!*, directed by Richard Lester. Scenes showing the Beatles recording their latest song were shot at Knighton Down, near Larkhill army base. The group stayed at the Antrobus Arms Hotel, Amesbury, and were driven to their location each day in a black Austin Princess limousine. Huge crowds of teenagers blocked the street through Amesbury trying to catch a glimpse of them. The *Salisbury Journal* reported that the limo was left unlocked in the hotel garage during the day and fans looted it for Beatles' souvenirs, such as caps, items of Beatles' clothing, even emptying the ashtrays of Beatles' cigarette butts.

A GREAT LOSS TO ROCK 'N' ROLL

Eddie Cochran (1938–1960), aka 'James Dean with a guitar', died on 17 April at St Martin's Hospital, Bath, from severe brain injury following a road accident on Rowden Hill, Chippenham, late on 16 April 1960. Cochran had been appearing at Bristol Hippodrome on the final stage of his UK tour with Gene Vincent. In the car were his girlfriend, Sharon Sheeley, tour manager, Pat Thompkins, and taxi-driver, George Martin. The car supposedly blew a tyre and crashed into a lamp post. Vincent suffered severe leg injuries while the others were uninjured.

One of the first policemen at the scene of the accident was a young Wiltshire police cadet, David Harman, who later changed his name to Dave Dee, becoming a highly successful pop star with his band Dave Dee, Dozy, Beaky, Mick & Tich. It is said that Harman retrieved Cochran's guitar from the wreck, later returning it to the family but not before enjoying 'a good strum'.

There is a memorial stone to Cochran on Rowden Hill and an annual Eddie Cochran Festival held in Chippenham every April.

WILTSHIRE HAS MORE TALENT

Chris Barber, jazz trombonist and bandleader, lives at Chilton Foliat. He formed his first group, the Barber New Orleans Band, in 1949. In 1953, along with Monty Sunshine and Lonnie Donegan, he joined forces with Ken Colyer. In 1954 he created his own Chris Barber's Jazz Band, which has continued to be one of Europe's most successful traditional jazz bands, clocking up over 10,000 concerts.

James Blunt (Blount), singer and musician who achieved international success with the song 'You're Beautiful' (2004), was born into an army family in Tidworth. He was an officer in the Life Guards and served with the NATO peacekeeping force in Kosovo, 1999. Other duties included standing guard at The Queen's Mother's funeral in 2002. He left the Army soon after to pursue a musical career. *Back to Bedlam* (2003), his debut album, sold over 11 million copies, and his second album, *All the Lost Souls* (2007), went Gold in the UK after only four days. He was Best British Male Solo Artist and Best Pop Act awards at the Brit Awards in 2006, and Hottest Male in the Virgin Media Music Awards 2010.

Iona Brown, violinist and conductor, was born in Salisbury and lived in Bowerchalke from 1968 until her death in 2004. Her 1972 recording of 'The Lark Ascending' by Vaughan Williams is regarded as one of the finest interpretations. She worked with Otto Klemperer in the Philharmonia Orchestra, with Sir Neville Marriner's Academy of St Martin in the Fields and was Artistic Director of the Los Angeles Chamber Orchestra from 1987 to 1992. She was appointed OBE in 1986 and received the Knight of First Class Merit from King Harald of Norway for her work as Music and Artistic Director of the Norwegian Chamber Orchestra.

'The man should have his own blue plaque.' *NME*, January 2011.
Julian Cope, musician, poet, author, former frontman of The Teardrop Explodes and expert on Neolithic stones lives near Avebury. He is the author of *The Modern Antiquarian* (1998) and *The Megalithic European* (2004).

Jamie Cullum, jazz musician and singer-songwriter, was brought up in Hullavington, educated at Grittleton House School and Sheldon School, Chippenham. He produced his first album *Jamie Cullen Trio – Heard it all Before* in 1999 himself for £48 but it was 'Pointless Nostalgia' (2002) which caught the ear of Michael Parkinson who promoted him his BBC TV chat show. His *Twentysomething* (2004) album sold 2.5million copies and became the fastest-selling jazz album in UK history.

Rick Davies, songwriter, musician and founder of rock band Supertramp, was born in Swindon and lived at No. 43 Eastcott Hill. He joined the British Railways Staff Association Brass and Silver Jubilee Band, and at Swindon Art College formed his own band, Rick's Blues. After a spell as a welder at a factory on Cheney Manor Trading Estate, he joined The Lonely Ones and went on tour to Europe in 1967. Supertramp was formed in 1969 with Roger Hodgson, Dougie Thomson, John Helliwell and Bob Siebenberg.

Their biggest-selling album was *Breakfast in America* (1979) which sold more than 20 million copies. Princess Diana was a fan and met the band in 1986. They performed at the Diana Tribute Concert in Wembley Stadium on 1 July 2007 in front of 63,000 people and broadcast to 140 countries around the world.

David Fanshawe, composer, explorer and ethnomusicologist, famous for his choral work *African Sanctus* (first broadcast on BBC Radio on United Nations Day 1972) moved to Aldbourne in 1992. He also wrote TV scores for *When the Boat Comes In* (1976–1981) and *Flambards* (1979).

Gerald Finzi, composer, lived at Beech Knoll, Aldbourne, with his wife, artist and poet Joyce Black, and wrote his famous *Dies Natalis* during this period. He was an avid book collector (his substantial collection bequeathed to Reading University), grew rare breed apples and promoted the works of composer and poet, Ivor Gurney.

Charles William Fry, bricklayer, musician and founder of the first Salvation Army Band, was born in Alderbury. He led an orchestra and band at the Wesleyan Chapel and helped at the Christian Mission, Salisbury. In 1878, Charles and his three sons, Fred, Ernest and Bert, started the first Salvation Army brass band in Salisbury taking part in open-air meetings in the Market Place. They accompanied Salvation Army founder William Booth in his evangelism campaigns until 1882, when the band ceased on his death.

Peter Gabriel, rock musician, former lead singer of rock band, Genesis, record producer and founder of the WOMAD (World of Music, Arts and Dance) Festival, lives in Corsham. He launched his own record label and recording studio between 1986 and 1988, located at his Real World Studios in a 200-year-old converted water mill in Mill Lane, Box. His bestselling, multi-platinum awarded album *So* (1986) was ranked as number fourteen by the *Rolling Stone* magazine's 'Top 100 Albums of the Eighties'.

David 'Dave Dee' Harman, musician and frontman of the 1960s chart toppers Dave Dee, Dozy, Beaky, Mick & Tich (aka DDDBMT) was born in Salisbury as were the other original members John Dymond (Beaky) and Ian Amey (Tich). Trevor Ward-Davies (Dozy) was born in Enford, and Michael Wilson (Mitch) in Amesbury. Their biggest hit was 'The Legend of Xanadu' (from their album *If No One Sang*) which reached number one in 1968.

Justin Hayward, musician and lead singer with the Moody Blues, was born in Dean Street, Swindon, and went to Commonweal Grammar School. He sang in the choir of St Saviour's Church and performed in several Swindon bands before joining the Moody Blues in 1966. The group has sold more than 55 million records. Hayward wrote their signature song 'Nights in White Satin', and 'Tuesday Afternoon' was inspired by visits to Lydiard Park as a child.

Nicky James (Michael Nichols) (1943–2007), musician and the leading force in Brumbeat, the West Midlands music scene during the 1960s, was a songwriter in partnership with groups such as The Hollies and the Moody Blues. He moved to Aldbourne in the 1970s where he founded Stables Studio.

Madonna Ciccone, singer, lived at Ashcombe House, Tollard Royal, with Guy Ritchie, the film director, between 2000 and 2008.

In 2013, one of the best-selling and most critically acclaimed albums of all times, Pink Floyd's *The Dark Side of the Moon* celebrated its fortieth anniversary. Pink Floyd drummer, Nick Mason, lives at Middlewick House, Corsham, which he bought from Andrew and Camilla Parker-Bowles in 1995.

Gilbert O'Sullivan, singer-songwriter, was born in Waterford, Ireland, and lived in Swindon from 1953 to 1967, attending St Joseph's Secondary Modern and Swindon College of Art. He played with fellow student Rick Davies (*see* entry above) in his band Rick's Blues. He got his big break when John Peel gave him a slot on his BBC Radio 1 show *Top Gear*. 'Nothing Rhymed' was his first top ten hit (1970) reaching number eight. 'Alone Again (Naturally)' (1972) reached number three, and 'Clair' reached number one in 1973. His album *Back to Front* (1972) remained in the UK album charts for sixty-four weeks, reaching number one. He was named Songwriter of the Year in 1973, and his song 'Get Down' won Best Song of the Year in 1974.

Andy Sheppard, jazz saxophonist and composer, was born in Warminster and attended Bishop Wordsworth's Grammar School, Salisbury. He started playing with Bristol-based quartet Sphere when he was nineteen. He was named Best Newcomer at the British Jazz Awards in 1987, followed by Best Instrumentalist in 1988 and 1989.

Ian Scott Anderson, musician, flautist and frontman to rock band Jethro Tull moved to Minety, near Malmesbury, in 1994. The band released thirty studio and live albums, selling more than 60 million copies since their formation in 1968. He was appointed MBE in 2007 for services to music.

Gordon Sumner, aka Sting, musician, songwriter and lead singer of rock band Police, was listed ninth in the 2011 Top 50 Music Millionaires. He is married to Trudie Styler, actress, director and businesswoman. They have a home in New York and own a 165-acre organic farm at Lake House Farm, Wilsford-cum-Lake, near Salisbury.

Regarded as one of England's greatest composers since Elgar, Michael Tippett (1905–1998) lived at No. 38 High Street, High Corsham, during the 1960s, and at Nocketts Hill Farm in Derry Hill from 1970 to 1996. Notable works include *A Child in Our Time*, *The Midsummer Marriage* and *The Knot Garden*. He was knighted in 1966 and appointed to the Order of Merit in 1983.

Midge Ure, rock musician with Thin Lizzy and former frontman for Ultravox, lives in Monkton Farlaigh. He co-wrote the Band Aid hit 'Do They Know it's Christmas'.

Toyah Wilcox, singer and actress, is married to guitarist Robert Fripp, founder of rock band King Crimson. They lived at Reddish House, Broad Chalke, the former home of photographer and designer, Cecil Beaton. In 2001, she was voted number forty-eight in *Q* magazine's 'Top 100 Greatest Women in Music' poll.

Swindon's own home-grown British New Wave rock group XTC began in 1972 with Andy Partridge (guitar and vocals) and Colin Moulding (bass and vocals) under the name Star Park. Their first gig was at Swindon College as support to Thin Lizzy. They became Helium Kidz, and Terry Chambers (drums) joined them in 1973, along with ex-King Crimson Barry Andrews (keyboard) when they became XTC in 1976. Dave Gregory replaced Andrews in 1979. Their debut album was *White Music* (1978), which was recorded in one week. Their single 'Making Plans for Nigel' (1979) reached number seventeen in the charts, and 'Senses Working Overtime' (1982) reached number ten.

BROADCAST SOUNDS

Daphne Oram (1925–2003),the first composer of electronic music in Britain, was born in Ivy House, Devizes. She started at the BBC in 1943 and founded the BBC's Radiophonic Workshop in 1957. She created and produced background music and sound effects to programmes such as BBC's *Quatermass and the Pit* (1959) and *Doctor Who* (1963) creating the signature tune with Delia Derbyshire. She invented the Oramics Machine in the early 1960s, which enabled musicians to 'draw' and arrange synthetic sounds.

'We've Only Just Begun' by The Carpenters was the first record played on the first breakfast show presented by Paul Chantler on BBC Wiltshire Sound's launch on 4 April 1989. Home Secretary and Wiltshire resident Rt Hon. Douglas Hurd officially opened the station and unveiled a plaque carved by stonemason John Lloyd from Great Bedwyn.

Radio engineer and broadcaster Quentin Howard recorded birdsong in his back garden in West Lavington in 1991, for a production of *When the Wind Blows* by Raymond Briggs. His recordings were aired again eighteen hours a day from July to September 1992 on Radio Birdsong, part of test transmissions for the new national radio station Classic FM, built by Howard.

In 1999, Howard created Digital One, UK's first national commercial DAB network, and the birdsong tapes were used yet again for a few weeks prior to launch. Steve Jones, a fan of Radio Birdsong, claimed to have identified twelve types of birds, including great-tits, greenfinches, wrens, swallows and flycatchers. Radio Birdsong is now available on the internet.

11

STAGE, SCREEN & TV

SHOWBIZ NEWS

Shakespeare's Company, The Lord Chamberlain's Men, are believed to have performed in the courtyard of The White Hart, Marlborough, in the 1690s.

'Signior Scaglioni, proprietor of the Original Dancing Dogs, which have performed 600 nights at Sadler's Wells, and at the Theatre Royal, Dublin, Edinburgh, York, Manchester, Birmingham, Bath ... and other major principal towns in England, intends to exhibit at the Theatre in New Street (Salisbury) on 5 August, and every other evening in the Race week.' (*Salisbury & Winchester Journal*, 21 July 1788)

An up-and-coming young comedian, Charlie Chaplin, appeared on the same bill as Marie Lloyd, Harry Lauder and George Robey at The Palace Theatre, Salisbury, around 1905.

In 1910, Aldbourne resident and dramatist Chares McEvoy converted the malthouse in South Street into a theatre and put on his new play, *The Village Wedding* – a cottage drama in three acts. A host of celebrities attended, including George Bernard Shaw, Edgar Wallace and Granville Barker. The amateur actors went on tour around the region finishing with a performance in London's Coronet Theatre on 29 May. Sadly, the run was cut short, possibly due to the audience's failure to understand the Wiltshire dialect.

Film actor David Niven (1910–1983) married Primula Rollo at her local church of St Nicholas, Huish, near Pewsey, on 21 September 1940. She was a member of the Women's Auxiliary Air Force when she met Lieutenant Niven of the Rifle Brigade. They moved to New York in April 1946, following the birth of their second son.

Primula died on 21 May 1946 after accidentally falling down stone steps to the cellar at Tyrone Power's house. She had mistaken the door for a closet during a party game of hide and seek. She is buried in the churchyard of St Nicholas.

Colonel Victor Cazalet MC (1896–1943), MP for Chippenham between 1924 and 1943, and four times Amateur Squash Champion (1925/27/29/30), was godfather to Hollywood star Elizabeth Taylor. He gave her a New Forest pony called Betty for her fifth birthday. He died in a plane crash while accompanying Polish leader General Sikorski on a visit to the Polish forces in the Middle East.

Hollywood star Greta Garbo used to visit her friend photographer and designer Cecil Beaton at his home Reddish House, Broad Chalke, where he lived from 1948 to 1980. She enjoyed shopping in Salisbury market and the freedom of walking the Downs unrecognised.

In 1988, Dents of Warminster made gloves for Michael Keeton's Batman and Jack Nicholson's the Joker in the Warner Bros film *Batman* (1989).

Hollywood actress Goldie Hawn stayed at the Ivy House Hotel, Marlborough, in July 2000 when she came over to visit the region. She chartered a plane with a group of fellow Americans to view crop circles around Avebury.

Sir David 'Del Boy' Jason is patron of the Association of Air Ambulances and visited the Wiltshire Air Ambulance at Devizes police headquarters on 22 September 2010 to celebrate its twentieth anniversary.

THE SIREN OF SWINDON

'I'm the kind of girl that things happen to. When they don't, I give them a push.' Diana Dors (1931–1984), actress and film star who was promoted as the 'English Marilyn Monroe', was born Diana Mary Fluck in Haven Nursing Home, Kent Road in Swindon. The family lived at No. 210, Marlborough Road, and her father worked in accounts at the Swindon GWR Works. She attended Selwood House School in Swindon and aged fourteen became the youngest ever student at the London Academy of Music and Dramatic Art (LAMDA), having lied about her age to enrol. She changed her name, using her grandmother's maiden name Dors, and dyed her hair blonde. At sixteen, she was under contract to the Rank Organisation.

First and Last Film
Her first film was *Shop at Sly Corner* (1947) with Oscar Homolka, and her first starring role was in *Diamond City* (1949), she was a late replacement for Jean Kent. Her last was in *Steaming* (1985) directed by Joseph Losey, starring alongside Vanessa Redgrave and Sarah Miles.

The Film That Made Her Name
Lady Godiva Rides Again (1951), starring Dennis Price, John McCallum and Stanley Holloway, caused such a stir with Diana's navel on display in one scene, that the American Board of Film censors temporarily banned it for being too risqué.

Money and Cars
Dors was so successful that at seventeen she was able to buy her first car, a sky-blue 1949 Delahaye Roadster 175S, one of only 150 made, for £5,000 (equivalent to £113,000 in 2005) before even passing her driving test. The car was sold in 2010 for £2 million. At twenty, she became the youngest registered owner of a Rolls-Royce in the UK.

Deadly Connection
Ruth Ellis, the last woman to be hanged for murder in Britain in 1955, had a walk-on part as a beauty queen contestant in *Lady Godiva Rides Again* (1951). Dors knew Ruth Ellis from the London club scene where they became friends. Dors later appeared in *Yield to the Night* (1956) as a convicted murderer, mistakenly said to have been based on the Ruth Ellis case, but in fact came from the book by Joan Henry written two years before.

Marriages
Dennis Hamilton Gittins	1951–1959	died
Richard (Dickie) Dawson	1959–1966	divorced; two sons
Alan Lake	1968–1984	one son (Lake took his own life five months after Dors' death)

Awards
In 1956 she was voted the Variety Club's 'Show Business Personality of the Year' and her new film, *Yield to the Night*, was chosen for the Royal Command Film Performance. She appeared twice on *This is Your Life* (1957 and 1982) and twice on Radio 4's *Desert Island Discs* (1961 and 1981). Her favourite disc both times was Ravel's 'Pavane pour une infant défunte'.

Beatles Connection

A personal favourite of John Lennon, Diana Dors appeared among the Beatles' heroes on Peter Blake's iconic album cover for 'Sgt Pepper's Lonely Hearts Club Band' (1967).

Three Lookalikes

A bust by Enid G.D. Mitchell FRBS (1988) used to take pride of place in the foyer of the Wyvern Theatre, Swindon, but is currently kept in their archives.

A life-size bronze statue by John Clinch was unveiled in June 1991 outside Shaw Ridge Entertainment Centre, Swindon.

Naomi Dors (formerly Polley) from Sunderland is the only Diana Dors lookalike in the UK. She works as The Northeast England Diana Dors Style Singing Telegram. She won the Diana Dors Competition at the Queen's Park Fun Day in Swindon in July 2009.

DOCTOR WHO CONNECTIONS

Devizes auctioneer Henry Aldridge & Son sold a full-size model of a Dalek from an early episode of the first BBC series of *Doctor Who* for £600 on 19 November 2011.

Born John Anthony Woods, in West Harnham in Salisbury, actor John Levene, appeared in seventy-three episodes of *Doctor Who* between 1967 and 1975, opposite Jon Pertwee. He started as a Yeti and then moved through the ranks from Corporal to Regimental Sergeant Major Benton of the special military force UNIT in episodes including 'Inferno', 'The Claws of Axos', 'The Dæmons' and 'Terror the Zygons'.

Billie Piper, born Leanne Piper, the actress and former singer, was born in Swindon. She was the youngest ever artist to debut at number one in the UK singles chart, with 'Because We Want To' (1998). She played

Rose Tyler in thirty-four episodes of *Doctor Who*, companion to the ninth Doctor, Christopher Eccleston, and to the tenth Doctor, David Tennant. She won 'Most Popular Actress' award in the National Television Awards in 2005, and *Hello* magazine's award for 'Most Attractive Woman' in 2011.

Cyril Luckham (1907–1989), TV, film and stage actor, was born in Salisbury. He played the White Guardian in *Doctor Who*. He played Archbishop Thomas Cranmer in *A Man for all Seasons* (1966) and Prior Houghton in *Anne of a Thousand Days* (1969). He played Dr Tinsley in several early episodes of *Coronation Street*, Sir Lawrence Mont in *The Forsyte Saga* (1967) and Bishop Grantley in *The Barchester Chronicles* (1982).

Victoria Wicks, the actress who played Sally Smedley in *Drop the Dead Donkey* (1990–1998), played the High Priestess of the Sybillines in *Doctor Who* (2008). She was born in Chippenham in 1959. Her mother's father was author H.E. Bates who wrote *The Darling Buds of May*.

BORN IN WILTSHIRE

Oh, Brother

Felix Aylmer, stage, screen and TV actor, who played Prior Father Anselm in *Oh Brother!*, was born in Corsham in 1889. His long career included roles such as Archbishop of Canterbury in Olivier's *Henry V* in 1947, Polonius in Olivier's *Hamlet* in 1948, and Gascoigne Quilt in the TV series *The Walrus and the Carpenter* in 1965. He was knighted in 1965.

Are You Free?

Trevor Bannister (1934–2011) stage, screen and TV actor, best known for his role as ladies' man Mr Lucas in BBC TV series *Are You Being Served?* (1972–1985), was born and brought up in Durrington. He made his West End debut in *Billy Liar* with Albert Finney and went on to make more than 500 TV appearances, in programmes such as *Z Cars* (1969), *The Dustbin Men* (1970), *Tomorrow's People* (1975), *Wyatt's Watchdogs* (1988) and latterly *Coronation Street (*2006) and *Last of the Summer of Wine* (2010).

Ooh, Betty!

Born Michael Dumbell-Smith in Salisbury in 1942, Michael Crawford, actor and singer, made his name as Frank Spencer in BBC TV sitcom *Some Mothers Do 'Ave 'Em* (1973–1978) where he performed his own stunts. He went on to appear in musicals such as *Barnum* (1981) and *The Phantom of the Opera* (1986) – the album version selling over 12 million copies – and won many awards here and on Broadway. He was appointed OBE (1987). He moved to New Zealand in 2006 for health reasons but returned to the West End to play the Wizard of Oz in 2011/12.

And Now the News

Broadcaster and BBC Home Service radio announcer Ronald Fletcher (1910–1996) was born in Salisbury. On 10 July 1948, he announced the betrothal of Princess Elizabeth to Lieutenant Philip Mountbatten. He appeared on *Breakfast with Braden* and *Bedtime with Braden* in the 1950s and *Round the Bend* with Michael Bentine (1957). Nigel Rees chose him to read the quotations for BBC Radio 4's *Quote... Unquote* in 1975, which he continued to do for the first 200 episodes.

Sitting Tenant

Mark Lamarr, radio DJ and TV presenter, was born in Swindon and went to Park School (now Oakfield). In the 1990s he co-presented Channel 4's *The Word*, and chaired *Never Mind the Buzzcocks* from 1996 to 2005.

Married to Magnum PI

Jillie Mack, actress and dancer, was born in Devizes. She married Hollywood actor Tom Selleck, star of *Magnum PI*, *Three Men and a Baby* and *Blue Bloods*, in August 1987 at the Cherrywood Waterfall Chapel in Lake Tahoe, Nevada.

The Bare Facts

Melinda Messenger, former *Sun* Page 3 Girl turned TV presenter, was born in Swindon. She appeared in *Celebrity Big Brother* in 2002, the Christmas Panto in Birmingham in 2003, and presented *Bingo Night Live* in 2008 and co-hosts *Cowboy Builders* presently. Her husband, Wayne Roberts, runs an electronics business in Swindon and they lived near Wanborough for a while before moving. She became an ambassador for Barnardo's in 2009, opening a new Children's Centre in Cricklade, June 2010. She opened a new Breast Screening Centre in Swindon, March 2010.

QI Regular

David Mitchell, actor, comedian and writer, and star of *Mitchell and Webb*, *Peep Show* and *Would I Lie to You?*, was born in Salisbury where his parents were hotel managers.

Larger than Life

Robert Morley (1908–1992), actor and playwright, was born in Semley near Tisbury. His first stage success was in the title role of *Oscar Wilde* (1936) in London and on Broadway. In his first film, *Marie Antoinette* (1938), he portrayed Louis XVI opposite Norma Shearer and appeared in *The African Queen* (1951), *Topkapi* (1964) and *The Human Factor* (1979). He was appointed CBE in 1957 but declined a knighthood in 1975.

HARRY POTTER CONNECTIONS

The main hall and medieval cloisters of Lacock Abbey, home of the pioneering photographer William Henry Fox Talbot (1800–1877), is now owned by the National Trust and appeared in the 'Harry Potter' films as Hogwarts School of Wizardry and Witchcraft. Cantax Hill, Church Street and the Sign of the Angel in the village have also appeared as locations.

Harry Potter's most famous form of transport from 'Platform 9¾', King's Cross Station, is the steam locomotive the Hogwarts Express. The GWR 'Hall' Class 4-6-0 No.5972 engine was originally built in Swindon in 1937 rescued from a scrapyard in the 1970s and carefully restored and renamed.

Harry Potter and the Order of the Phoenix (2007), *Harry Potter and the Half-Blood Prince* (2009), *Harry Potter and the Deathly Hallows Part 1* (2010) and *Harry Potter and the Deathly Hallows Part 2* (2011) were directed by David Yates, who started his career at Cree8 Studios, Regent Circus in Swindon. His first film, *When I Was a Girl* (1988), was shot in Swindon where he was living in Ferndale Road, Gorse Hill, at the time. Yates received a grant from Thamesdown Media Arts to help fund the work.

Ralph Fiennes played Lord Voldermort in *Harry Potter and the Goblet of Fire*, *Harry Potter and the Order of the Phoenix* and *Harry Potter and the Deathly Hallows Part 1 & Part 2*. He attended Bishop Wordsworth's School in Salisbury from 1976 to 1981, where he played Thomas Cromwell in a school production of *A Man For All Seasons*.

Swindon-born Melanie Byrne is a visual effects producer. Her work includes *Harry Potter and the Order of the Phoenix* (2007), *Chronicles of Narnia: The Voyage of the Dawn Treader* (2010) and BBC TV series *Call the Midwife* (2012).

FIVE OLD MARLBURIANS

Frank Gardner, BBC security correspondent, journalist and author, attended Marlborough College from 1974 to 1979. He studied Arabic and Islamic Studies at Exeter University and started at the BBC in 1995, later becoming their first full-time Gulf correspondent. In June 2004, while on assignment in Saudi Arabia, he was shot six times at close range, and given only a 10 per cent chance of survival. Severely wounded he is now dependant on a wheelchair but has continued working and travelling around the world. He was appointed OBE in 2005.

'Upper-class gentlemen and affable rogue' actor Wilfrid Hyde-White (1903–1991) attended Marlborough College and RADA. He appeared in *The Browning Version* (1951), *The Reluctant Debutante* (1955), *Two-Way Stretch* (1960), *My Fair Lady* (1964), US TV series *Ben Casey* (1961–1966) and *The Associates* (1979–80). In the BBC radio comedy series *The Men from Ministry* (1962–1965), he played the character Number One in the General Assistance Department of an unnamed government ministry in Whitehall, alongside Richard Murdoch.

David Nobbs, writer and creator of Reggie Perrin, attended Marlborough College. He began his comedy career in 1963 as a contributor to *That Was the Week that Was*. In the BBC's *The Fall and Rise of Reginald Perrin* (1976–1979) he gave us memorable lines such as 'I didn't get where I am today by ...', 'There's no smoke without the worm turning' and 'It's the early bird that catches the quick brown fox'. And oh, of course, the two office Yes-men's 'Great!' and 'Su-per!'

James Mason (1909–1984), actor, was born in Yorkshire and attended Marlborough College. He won a Golden Globe for 'Best Motion Picture Actor' for his work in the film *A Star is Born* (1954) and was three times Oscar-nominated for *A Star is Born*, *Gregory's Girl* (1966) and *The Verdict* (1982).

James Robertson Justice (1907–1975), actor, was born in Lewisham and attended Marlborough College. He was best known for his role as Sir Lancelot Spratt in the 'Doctor' films: *Doctor in the House* (1954); *Doctor at Sea* (1955); *Doctor at Large* (1957); *Doctor in Love* (1960); *Doctor in Distress* (1963); *Doctor in Clover* (1966) and *Doctor in Trouble* (1970). His biography *What's the Bleeding Time?* was published in 2008.

OTHERS WITH WILTSHIRE CONNECTIONS

The George Baker Centre, home of West Lavington Youth Club, commemorates the work of village resident George Baker (1931–2011), actor, writer and director who is best known for his portrayal of Chief Inspector Wexford in the 'Ruth Rendell' Mysteries. He appeared in more than thirty films including *The Dam Busters* (1955) and *On Her Majesty's Secret Service* (1969), having once been considered for the lead in the first James Bond film. He appeared on TV as Stanley Bowler in *Bowler* (1973), Tiberius in *I, Claudius* (1976) and Login in four episodes of *Doctor Who* (1980). He was appointed MBE in 2007 for his charity work with young people.

Actor Roy Dotrice twice portrayed seventeenth-century antiquary and writer John Aubrey (born 1626 in Earston Pierse near Malmesbury) first in a stage adaptation of *Brief Lives* (1967) and later on BBC TV – 'It is a cold winter's day in 1696. John Aubrey is recounting his sometimes bawdy, sometimes instructive, and always entertaining gossip that he has been collecting all his life.'

'You don't have to say anything but …' Stephen Fry, actor, writer and broadcaster, was arrested in the Wiltshire Hotel in Swindon on 9 September 1975 for credit card fraud. He spent the night in the cells at Swindon police station and appeared before local magistrates the next morning. He was remanded in custody and taken by van to Pucklechurch near Bristol, a remand prison for young offenders. He remained there for three months before being sentenced, receiving a probation order. He wrote about this in his autobiography *Moab is My Washpot* (1997).

Pioneering filmmaker John Grierson (1898–1972) lived at Tog Hill, the former miller's house which he restored, in Calstone Wellington near Calne, from 1951 until his death. He coined the word 'documentary' to describe non-fiction films in 1926. His best known work was *Night Mail* (1936) produced and narrated with Stuart Legg, which included W.H. Auden's specially written poem and Benjamin Britten score. He established the National Film Board of Canada during the Second

World War. The Grierson Awards for documentary makers home and abroad were established in 1972.

James Grout (1927–2012), TV and film actor, moved to Malmesbury in 1977. He wrote a regular column for the *Wiltshire Gazette and Herald* in the 1980s. He won a scholarship to RADA but his training was interrupted by National Service with the RAF in Wiltshire, where he trained as a radar mechanic, managing to keep up the acting in amateur theatricals held in one of the aircraft hangars. He performed at the Old Vic and with the RSC and acted with John Thaw in *Redcap* (1964–1966) and in *Inspector Morse* (1987–2000) where he played Chief Superintendent Strange. He was a veteran of Radio 4's *King's Street Junior* and *Old Harry's Game*.

Christine Hamilton, aka the 'British Battleaxe', TV personality and author, lives at Bradfield Manor, Hullavington – once the property of Eton College (1443–1958) – with Neil Hamilton, barrister and Conservative MP for Tatton (1983–1997).

Sheila Hancock, actor, director and author, moved to a seventeenth-century manor house in Luckington (or Lucky as she calls it) in 1990 with husband John Thaw (1942–2002), the actor famous for playing the lead role in the TV series *Inspector Morse*.

Andrew Harvey, broadcaster and journalist, attended Bishop Wordsworth's School from 1957 to 1962. He presented BBC's *South Today*, the *Nine O'clock News*, and also on the ITV News Channel.

David Hemmings (1941–2003), actor, lived in the Old Mill, Calne for a number of years, and after his death on location in Romania in 2003, was buried at St Peter's Church, Blacklands, Calne.

BBC *Flog It!* host Paul Martin, an antiques expert and TV presenter, lives in Seend.

Entrepreneur and dragon on BBC's *Dragon's Den* Deborah Meaden attended Dauntsey's School and Trowbridge High School.

Christopher Miles, film director and brother of actress Sarah Miles, moved to Calstone Wellington near Calne in 1993. He is best known for *Up Jumped a Swagman* (1965), *Virgin and the Gypsy* (1970) and *Priest of Love* (1981). He helped to raise over £1,000 towards the restoration of the 300-year-old Royal Coat of Arms above the chancel at St Mary the Virgin Church in Calstone.

Keen narrowboaters since 1979, actor Timothy West (vice-president of The Waterways Trust and the Kennet & Avon Canal Trust) and wife, actress Prunella Scales, have sponsored a bench on a section of the Kennet & Avon Canal. When the canal reopened in August 1990, their boat was the first to travel the entire length of the Kennet & Avon Canal, except for a 400-yard stretch (including lock 43) at the summit of the Caen Hill flight, which had been reserved for the Queen to open.

ROBOT WARS

Tom Gutteridge, TV producer and founder of Mentorn, Britain's largest independent production company, lived at The Old Manor in Market Lavington. He was responsible for programmes such as *Challenge Anneka* and *Question Time*, and the man behind the British version of *Robot Wars* (1998–2004). In 2002 he supported the local Queen's Golden Jubilee fete by bringing along Sir Killalot, star of the show, to open the event.

12

FILM FILE

FILMS WITH WILTSHIRE LOCATIONS

1918	*Hearts of the World*, Salisbury Plain
1924	*Tess of the D'Urbevilles*, Stonehenge
1927	*The Somme*, Salisbury Plain
1933	*A Cuckoo in the Nest*, Red Lion Inn, Avebury
1941	*Kipps*, Lacock
1943	*The Way Ahead*, Salisbury Plain
1949	*The Small Back Room*, Stonehenge
1950	*The Elusive Pimpernel*, Savernake Forest and Marlborough Downs
1951	*The Magic Box*, Lacock
1958	*The Night of the Demon*, Stonehenge
	The Moonraker, Lacock Abbey and village and Stonehenge
1960	*The Grass is Greener*, Lacock Abbey
1963	*The Tomb of Ligeia*, Stonehenge
1964	*Guns at Batasi*, Salisbury Plain
1965	*Help!*, Knighton Down, near Salisbury; Larkhill, Stonehenge
	It Happened Here, Berwick St John, Salisbury
	The Secret of My Success, Stourhead and Lacock Abbey
	Catch Us If You Can, Salisbury Plain and Imber
1967	*Doctor Dolittle*, Castle Combe
	Far from the Madding Crowd, Vale of Pewsey; Devizes Corn Exchange; St John's Church
1971	*The Music Lovers*, Larmer Tree Gardens, Tollard Royal
1972	*Triple Echo*, Wylye Valley, Berwick St James
1973	*Lady Caroline Lamb*, Wilton House
1975	*Barry Lyndon*, Wilton House; Stourhead Gardens
1984	*Nineteen Eighty-Four*, Roundway Hill, Devizes; hangar at RAF Hullavington

	The Bounty, Double-Cube Room, Wilton House
	Hawkwind: The Solstice at Stonehenge, Stonehenge
1985	*Return to Oz*, Chitterne, Salisbury Plain
	A View to a Kill, Norman Foster's Renault Building, Swindon
1987	*Maurice*, Wilbury Park, Newton Toney near Amesbury
1989	*Scandal*, Longleat
1991	*Robin Hood, Prince of Thieves*, Old Wardour Castle
1993	*The Remains of the Day*, Dyrham Park, Corsham Court
1994	*The Madness of King George*, Double-Cube Room, Wilton House
1995	*Sense and Sensibility*, Mompesson House, Salisbury; Trafalgar Park, near Salisbury; Double-Cube Room, Wilton House
1996	*Moll Flanders*, Lacock
	Portrait of a Lady, Heale House Gardens, near Salisbury
1997	*Mrs Brown*, Double-Cube Room, Wilton House
1998	*Saving Private Ryan*, Wiltshire Downs
	Still Crazy, Stone Circle and Red Lion Inn, Avebury
1999	*The World is not Enough*, Motorola's Groundwell Building, Swindon
	Milk, around Wiltshire
2000	*Chocolat*, Salisbury; Fonthill Lake, Fonthill Bishop
	Billy Elliott, new Wardour Castle
2001	*The Princess Diaries*, Longford Castle, Odstock
	Harry Potter and the Philosopher's Stone, Lacock Abbey and village
2002	*Harry Potter and The Chamber of Secrets*, Lacock Abbey and village
	28 Days Later, Trafalgar Park, near Salisbury
2003	*A Place to Stay*, Wiltshire
2004	*Kuch Din Kuch Pal (Any Day Any Time)*, Wilton Windmill
2005	*Pride and Prejudice*, Stourhead Garden; Double-Cube Room, Wilton House
2006	*Amazing Grace*, Trafalgar Park House, near Salisbury; Salisbury Cathedral
2007	*Stardust*, Castle Combe
2008	*The Other Boleyn Girl*, Great Chalfield Manor and Lacock Abbey
2009	*Harry Potter and Half-Blood Prince*, Lacock Abbey and village
	The Young Victoria, Wilton House
	Creation, Bradford on Avon

         Morris: a Life with Bells On, Tisbury
         Father of Girls, Salisbury
2010   *Patrol Men*, Salisbury
         The Drummond Will, Ramsbury and Baydon
         The Wolfman, Castle Combe, Lacock
2011   *War Horse*, Castle Combe, Lacock
2013   *Mariah Mundi and the Midas Box*, Lacock

TV FILMS AND PROGRAMMES WITH WILTSHIRE LOCATIONS

Tess, 1960 (ITV *Play of the Week*) Stonehenge, Salisbury Plain

Monitor (BBC) Ken Russell's *Debussy* (1965) Lamer Tree Gardens Tollard Royal; *Ralph Vaughan Williams* (1985) Stonehenge

Six Days to Saturday, 1963 (BBC) TV documentary, week in the life of Swindon Town FC. Director John Boorman

Pride and Prejudice, 1967 (BBC TV series) With Celia Bannerman, Lewis Flander. Lacock

Doctor Who, 'The Daemons', 1971 (BBC) Aldbourne as Devil's End, Ramsbury Airfield, Membury Airfield

Doctor Who, 'Planet of the Spiders', 1974 (BBC) Membury Airfield

The Pallisers, 1974 (BBC) Stourhead

Survivors, 1975–1977 (BBC) Series 3, episode 8, Imber on Salisbury Plain

Children of the Stones, 1977 (HTV) Avebury (representing fictional Milbury)

The Four Feathers, 1977 (NBC-TV film) Starring Robert Powell, Simon Ward, Beau Bridges. Littlecote House, Chilton Foliat and Wiltshire countryside

Blake 7, 1978–1981 (BBC) Corsham Cellars (former Pictor Monks Quarry)

Dick Turpin, 1979–1982 (LWT) Castle Combe

Shoestring, 1979–1980 (BBC) Swindon

Into the Labyrinth, 1980–1982 (TV series) 'book-end' shots, Avebury

Jobs on the Line, 1982 (BBC) Documentary on the threat to the future of Swindon Railway Works

Only Fools and Horses, 1981–1991 (BBC) Salisbury locations for street market and scenes in the boys' local pub

Robin Hood and the Sorcerer, 1983 (TV film with Michael Praed) Bowood House, Bradford on Avon, Tithe Barn and Lacock Abbey

Robin of Sherwood, 1984–1986 (HTV series) With Michael Praed. Azimghur Barracks, Colerne Airfield; Bradford on Avon, Tithe Barn; Bowood House; Castle Combe; Farleigh Hungerford Castle; Great Chalfield Manor House; Nettleton Mill and Lacock Abbey

Requiem for a Railway, 1985 (BBC) two-part documentary on closure of Swindon Railway Works

Off the Rails, 1986 (BBC) Documentary after the closure of Swindon Railway Works

Blackadder, Series 2, 1986 (BBC) Bridge and Gardens, Wilton House

The Day After the Fair, 1986 (BBC TV film) Salisbury, Mompesson House

Northanger Abbey, 1986 (BBC film) Bowood House Estate and Corsham Court

First Born, 1988 (BBC) Calne; Longleat Safari Park; New Wardour Castle; Savernake Forest

The Woman in Black, 1989 (BBC TV film) Lacock

Operation Solstice: the Battle of the Beanfield, 1991 (Channel 4 *Critical Eye* documentary)

Archer's Goon, 1992 (BBC) Salisbury

That's Football, 1994 (Channel 4) Documentary about Swindon Town FC under manager Glenn Hoddle) director Carl Ross

Pride and Prejudice, 1995 (BBC series) With Colin Firth, Jennifer Ehle. Lacock, Abbey and village; Luckington Court, Chippenham

Persuasion, 1995 (BBC TV film) Sheldon Manor, Chippenham (representing Upper Cross Great House)

Time Team Specials, 1995 (Channel 4) 'The Saxon Graves', Winterbourne Gunner and 'The Lost Villa', Tockenham

Return to Devil's End, 1996 (TV film) Aldbourne

Emma, 1996 (TV film) Lacock, Trafalgar Park House, near Salisbury

The Woodlanders, 1997 (Channel 4) Salisbury and Alvediston near Tisbury

Henry VIII, 1997 (TV mini-series) With David Starkey. Lacock

Tess of the D'Urbevilles, 1998, (ITV film) Stonehenge

Randall & Hopkirk (Deceased), 2000 (BBC) Lacock

The Murder of Roger Ackroyd, 2000 (ITV) Feature-length episode of *Poirot.* Castle Combe

Happy Birthday Shakespeare, 2000 (BBC) Salisbury Plain, Stonehenge

Animal Park, 2000–2009 (BBC) Longleat Safari Park

Blood of the Vikings, 2001 (BBC) Salisbury Plain

The Mayor of Casterbridge, 2003, Lacock

He Knew He Was Right, 2004 (BBC) Stourhead Gardens

Walk Away and I Stumble, 2005 (Granada TV film) Avebury Stone Circle; Calne, Chippenham

Beau Brummell, This Charming Man, 2006 (BBC TV film) Wilton House

Footprints in the Snow, 2005 (Channel 4/ITV drama) Salisbury Hospital and Salisbury

Time Team Special, 2005 (Channel4) Durrington Walls, Larkhill and Bulford

Tom Brown's Schooldays, 2005 (TV film) Red Lion Inn, Lacock

Walking with Shadows, 2006 (TV film) Marlborough

Persuasion, 2007 (BBC TV film) Great Chalfield Manor; Neston Park, Corsham; Sheldon Manor

Cranford, 2007 and 2009 (BBC) Lacock

Four Seasons (aka *Vier Jahreszeiten*), 2008 (Anglo-German TV mini-series based on a Rosamund Pilcher book) Longleat House; Neston Park, Corsham; Georgian manor house, New Wardour Castle

Tess of the D'Urbevilles, 2008 (BBC) Chippenham; Corsham and Corsham Court; Golden Ball Hill near Alton Barnes; Great Chalfield Manor; Kington St Michael; Lacock; Marlborough Downs above Lockeridge; Melksham; Shaw Farm near Marlborough; Stonehenge and Salisbury Plain

Lark Rise to Candleford, 2008–2011 (BBC) Hatt Farm, Box; Neston Park, Corsham

The Queen, the Life of the Monarch, 2009 (Channel4) Grittleton House, Chippenham; Longleat; Neston Park, Corsham; Stourhead House

Time Team Specials, 2009 (Channel4) 'The Secrets of Stonehenge', 'The Journey to Stonehenge', Durrington, and 'Buried Bishops and Belfries', Salisbury Cathedral

The Victorian Farm, 2009 (BBC) Wilton Windmill

Right Hand Drive, 2009 (Mark Kalbskopf) Bremhill, Chippenham, Kington St Michael

Doctor Who, 'The Pandorica Opens', 2010 (BBC) Stonehenge

Time Team: Potted History, 2010 (Channel4) Cunetio, Mildenhall

Mr Harvey Lights a Candle, 2011 (BBC film) Salisbury and Salisbury Cathedral

Roar, 2011 (CBBC) Longleat Safari and Adventure Park

Wild Britain with Ray Mears, 2013 (ITV) Salisbury Plain

Time Team: Warriors, 2013 (Channel4) Barrow Clump, Salisbury Plain

13

ANIMAL TALES

ALL YOU NEED TO KNOW ABOUT OUR COUNTY SYMBOL

'These plaines doe abound with hares, fallow deer, partridges and bustards'. (John Aubrey, *Natural History of Wiltshire*, 1656–1691)

The Great Bustard (Otis tarda) has been extinct as a breeding bird in Great Britain since 1832. Its demise has partly been attributed to the Victorians who were the first generation of ornithologists that started the craze for collecting specimens. In most countries, hunting of the males in the spring was only allowed so a big specimen could be obtained for the taxidermist.

There are four stuffed Great Bustards on display in the Salisbury and South Wiltshire Museum: the Maddington Hen and the Berwick St James cock, shot in 1871; a bird shot at Henswood near Marlborough in 1856; and a bird bought from Dinton House in 1917.

Four Facts
The bird has only three toes, which all point forward so that it is unable to perch. Adults males can weigh from 6 kilos up to 18 kilos. Wingspan can measure over 2.5m. Along with the Mute Swan and Kori Bustard of South Africa, it is one of the world's heaviest flying birds.

On the Table

Bustards were looked on as a delicacy for the dinner table by some, probably for their rarity and size, more than the actual quality of the meat – not very good!

The Great Bustard appeared on a special menu for King Richard III who was visiting Gainsborough Hall, Lincolnshire, in 1482:

  Baked pies of calves feet
  Whole side of roast beef
  Boiled rabbits with puddings
  Baked cranes and bustards
  White puddings of hogs liver
  Baked sparrow and other smaller birds
  Pestells (haunches) of red deer

A 1534 law of Henry VIII's protected Bustard eggs under the same penalty as those of the Crane – 'fine of twenty pence apiece'.

A 1543 law restricted 'luxurious feasting' and prohibited the Lord Mayor of London from buying 'either swan, crane, or bustard, under a penalty of 20s for every such bird'.

Born Again

The European Union gave £1.8 million in 2004 towards the Great Bustard Project on Salisbury Plain. A re-introduction programme was started with twenty-eight bustard chicks reared in Saratov Oblast in southern Russia. When the chicks were about six weeks old they were flown to the UK and after a period of quarantine were released on Salisbury Plain.

The Great Bustard was adopted as the symbol of Wiltshire for the county flag in June 2007.

The first Salisbury Plain chicks were born in 2009.

The current population is around twenty birds (2012).

Hengehogs by Simon Drew.

ALL SORTS

Antics

The Defence Science & Technology Laboratory reported: 'The uniquely high density of anthills in an area of Porton Down has led to its being known as the "antscape". Anthills are formed by the Yellow Meadow Ant lasius falvus. It has been estimated that there are 3 million anthills containing 35 billion ants on these grasslands.'

Never Tease a Tiger

A plaque in St Mary's Church, Hullavington, tells the story of Hannah Twyonny:

> She was a servant at the White Lion Inn, where was an Exhibition of Wild Beasts, and amongst the rest a very fierce tyger, which she imprudently took pleasure in teasing, notwithstanding the repeated remonstrance of its keeper. One day, whilst amusing herself with this dangerous diversion, the enraged animal, by extraordinary effort, drew out the staple, sprang towards the unhappy Girl, caught hold of her gown, and tore her to pieces.

Hannah Twyonny was buried in Malmesbury Abbey churchyard. Her gravestone reads:

In memory of
Hannah Twyonny
Who died October 23rd 1703
Aged 33 years
In bloom of life
She's snatched from hence
She had not room to make defence;
For Tyger fierce
took life away
And here she lies
In a bed of clay

Pat on the Back

Bruce, the Hospital Dog of Swindon, raised funds for the Victoria Hospital, Swindon. His owner, Arthur Beal, who worked in the Great Western Railway machine shop, took Bruce all around the South West with a collection box attached to a harness on the dog's back. A 1908 postcard of Bruce reads, 'I am Bruce of Swindon the famous Collecting Dog of nearly £500 for Charity. I have travelled 10,000 miles by rail. A solid Silver Collar, 16 Gold and Silver Medals have been Presented to me for my noble work. I am also a member of the Brotherhood of Hero Dogs London. My age is eight years, and for each coin I say Thank You.' Bruce died 23 July 1915 from an ulcerated stomach.

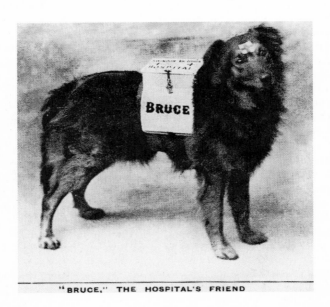

"BRUCE," THE HOSPITAL'S FRIEND

Bats in the Rafters

The Barn Gallery, Avebury, is home to five protected species of bats: Natterer's, Pipistrelle, Serotine, Brown Long-eared, and Soprano Pipistrelle.

Croppies Advice

Michael Glickman and Karen Alexander's *Crop Circle Etiquette* (2009), the pink book guidelines for visiting formations, includes sections on tramlines (keep to them), litter (don't), smoking (don't), what to wear (be prepared for the British weather), what to do about toilets (there are none) and dogs (leave at home). It reminds you of the unpredictability of animals and also 'there are many instances of dogs becoming ill in crop circles'. You have been warned.

THREE PIONEERS

Bird Migration

The first to identify the migration of some birds in winter to warmer climes was ornithologist John Legg (*c.* 1755–1802), who lived in Market Lavington and is buried at St Mary's Church. His *A Discourse on the Emigration of British Birds, Or, this Question at Last Solv'd: Whence Come the Stork and the Turtle, the Crane and the Swallow, when They Know and Observe the Appointed Time of Their Coming?* was published in 1780.

More Antics

Sir John Lubbock, Ist Baron Avebury (1834–1913), MP, banker, scientific writer and called 'the forgotten polymath' by *New Scientist* (1980) had interests including archaeology and zoology, and sponsored the Wild Birds Protection Act 1880. He tried to teach Van, his pet poodle, to read using a series of cards marked with words such as 'food', 'out' and 'water'. He kept a pet wasp which he took out and about to meetings, and kept a hive of bees and a colony of ants indoors to study. He was elected the first president of the

SIR JOHN LUBBOCK, M.P., F.R.S.

How doth the Banking Busy Bee
Improve his shining Hours
By studying on Bank Holidays
Strange Insects and Wild Flowers!

newly founded British Beekeepers Association in 1874.

He published a pioneering work on social insects called *Ants, Bees and Wasps: A Record of Observations on the Habits of the Social Hymenoptera* (1893). He was the first person to mark individual insects and managed to keep two particular ants to the ripe old age of fourteen and fifteen. He once got ants drunk to see what happened – 'they lay helplessly on their backs and the sober ants picked them up and carried them about in a sort of aimless way as if they did not know what to do with their drunkards.' Sound familiar?

Monkey (and Panda) Business

Desmond Morris, zoologist, anthropologist, artist and author, was born in Purton. He wrote *The Naked Ape* (1967), which has sold more than 12 million copies in twenty-three languages, and *The Human Zoo* (1969). He attended Dauntsey's School and lived in Swindon until 1951. He had his first solo art exhibition at Swindon Arts Centre in 1948 (and a retrospective at Swindon Public Art Gallery in 1993). During his National Service he was a lecturer in Fine Arts at Chiseldon Army College. He became Head of Granada TV and Film Unit at the Zoological Society London in 1956 and went on to become Curator of Mammals in 1959. He was responsible for bringing panda Chi-Chi (now stuffed and displayed in the Natural History Museum, London) to London Zoo and brokering the 'marriage' with Russia's An-An. The French editions of *Catwatching* and *Dogwatching* (1986) won the 'Prix Literaire de 30 Million Amis'.

Desmond Morris had a teenage fling with Swindon-born Diana Fluck (the future actress Diana Dors – *see* Stage, Screen & TV).

STUFFED, PRESERVED OR RECYCLED

The well-preserved corpse of an old English black rat which had traces of arsenic in it is on display at the Salisbury and South Wiltshire Museum. It was discovered curled up inside the skull of William Longespée (*c.* 1178–c1226), 3rd Earl of Salisbury, when his tomb in Salisbury Cathedral was opened in 1791 by architect James Wyatt during restoration work. It was rumoured that Longespée had been poisoned, this might account for the condition of the rat, but arsenic is also a preservative. The Earl was the illegitimate son of King Henry II and half-brother of King John. Longespée was one of the original witnesses to the Magna Carta and his wife, Ela, was the first abbess of

Lacock Abbey.

> A novel article of furniture may now be seen at Mr Ferris's, upholsterer, of this town (Devizes). It consists of a couch formed of the entire skin of the famous hunter Milkman', the property of the late Duke of Beaufort, and ridden by Will Long, his grace's huntsman, for 17 seasons. It is disposed in a kneeling position; and although the horse has been dead for some 8 or 10 years, several gentlemen acquainted with the Beaufort Hunt have recognised it as having once belonged to 'Milkman' – so well have the natural points which characterized the animal been preserved. (*Devizes Advertiser*, October 1860)

Bobbie of the Berkshires, the pet dog of Sergeant Kelly of the 66th Berkshire Regiment, survived the Battle of Maiwand, the Battle of Kandahar, and the return sea journey to England. Queen Victoria awarded him The Afghan War medal. Sadly, on 13 October 1882 he died in a road accident in Gosport. He was later stuffed and is now on display at The Rifles (Berkshire and Wiltshire) Museum, Salisbury.

Where's Horatio the Lion? In a glass case in the Wiltshire Heritage Museum, Devizes. The stuffed Lion has been around the block a bit, so to speak. In the early twentieth century he was owned by Mr Dickenson of Nursteed Road, Devizes, and has been displayed in shops such as EH Price's Music Shop (now Devizes's Books) and Sloper's (now Boots and Iceland). He also appeared on carnival floats and was wheeled around town to collect money for the Spitfire Fund during the Second World War.

ANIMALS AT WORK

For Fred Darling, master of Beckhampton Stables near Marlborough, 1927 was a good year for racing. His good fortune enabled him to build additional stables and exercise yard at Top Yard. No expense was spared on the eleven individual central heated wooden cage-boxes, with porcelain mangers and Minton-tiled walls, costing £1,200 each (equivalent to £35,000 in 2005).

TV presenter Johnny Morris (1916–1999), played the Hot Chestnut Man in *Playbox* (1953–1961), *Animal Magic* presenter (1962–1984), and the voice of *Tales of the Riverbank (*1960–1964) and *Further Tales* (1992), lived and worked in Aldbourne. He came to the village as a farm manager on a large estate belonging to art collector and stockbroker Jimmy Bomford. Morris broke into broadcasting in 1946 after being spotted by local resident Desmond Hawkins (broadcaster and founder of the BBC Natural History Unit) telling stories to friends in his local pub. He moved to Hungerford and died in a nursing home nearby and was buried in his 4-acre garden next to his wife.

Peregrine falcons are used by The Hills Group to frighten scavenging birds away from their local landfill sites.

Wadworth shire horses, Prince, Monty and Max take their annual holiday in the last two weeks of August in a field near Poulshot. The Devizes brewery has employed horses for over 100 years to deliver beer to local public houses and they still make daily visits around town. The horses work in pairs and pull a dray carrying a load weighing about two tons. Each horse weighs about 18cwts. Their daily feed consists of best hay, bran, molasses, brewer's grains and the occasional pint of 6X, Henry's IPA or Bishop's Tipple. A set of shoes lasts three weeks, and a mobile blacksmith visits weekly to keep them well shod.

In 2004, BBC TV made *The Legend of the Tamworth Two*, a film about two five-month-old Tamworth pigs, Butch and Sundance, which escaped the butcher's knife at Newman's abattoir in Malmesbury in 1998 and went on the run. It made headlines around the world and the pigs were eventually re-captured by *Daily Mail* reporters and bought from their owners. The pigs spent the rest of their days at an animal sanctuary in Ashford, Kent, but both animals had to be put down because of serious illnesses: Butch at aged thirteen in 2010 and Sundance at aged fourteen in 2011.

A Gold Medal was awarded to Wiltshire Police Force dog, Anya, a German Shepherd, on 6 July 2010, 'For devotion to duty and life-saving bravery in the face of danger, when faced with a knife-wielding assailant, on Thursday 14 January 2008.' Dog handler PC Neil Sampson and two colleagues were called to an incident in Liden, Swindon, where a man was brandishing a knife. Despite attempts to subdue the man, Anya and her handler were stabbed. PC Sampson needed surgery on his head and face and Anya received chest wounds from which she recovered. The man was sentenced to nine years for the attack.

14

ON THIS DAY

1 January 1870	Revd Francis Kilvert of Langley Burrell began his diary.
2 January 1940	King George VI paid an informal visit to Swindon to see troops in the Southern Command.
3 January 1797	Collapse of the southwest trilithon at Stonehenge, the first recorded fall of any stones.
4 January 1813	Sir Isaac Pitman, inventor of shorthand, was born in Trowbridge.
5 January 1996	Swindon-born David Hempleman-Adams became the first Briton to walk solo and unsupported to the South Pole.
6 January 1917	Strike meeting led by Florence Hancock over pay and conditions at Anglo-Swiss Dairy held at Temperance Hall, Chippenham.
7 January 1940	Test of all county Air Raid Warning Signals (except Salisbury) by Wiltshire Constabulary Police was held at 10 a.m.
8 January 1998	The Tamworth Two, two rare breed pigs called Butch and Sundance, escaped from Newman's abattoir, Malmesbury.
9 January 2009	Salisbury-born musician David (Dave Dee) Harman, lead singer of group Dave Dee, Dozy, Beaky, Mick and Titch, died aged sixty-five.
10 January 1914	Harold Fleming scored the only (winning) goal for Swindon Town FC v Man United in FA Cup first round.
11 January 1928	Thomas Hardy, novelist and poet, inspired by Wiltshire, died in Dorchester.
12 January 1952	*Gone to Earth*, starring Jennifer Jones and David Farrar is shown at the Savoy, Swindon.

13 January 1943	No. 511 Squadron, RAF Lyneham flew Prime Minister Winston Churchill to the Casablanca Conference to meet President Roosevelt and President Stalin.
14 January 1885	One of the 'Dynamite Outrages' bomb explosions damaged Warminster Town Hall. It turned out to be a 'prank' played by two local men, not the act of an Irish Republican group.
15 January 1972	Record attendance of 31,668 at the County Ground for the Swindon v Arsenal FA Cup tie – they lost 2–0.
16 January 1842	Flooding of River Till in Tilshead destroyed dozens of cottages.
17 January 1908	Swindon-born suffragette Edith New and her fellow suffragette Olivia Smith were arrested for chaining themselves to No. 10 Downing Street railings.
18 January 1980	Sir Cecil Beaton, photographer and designer, died at his home, Reddish House in Bowerchalke.
19 January 1942	Actor and singer Michael Crawford was born in Salisbury.
20 January 1954	Crew of four died when a Vickers Varsity crashed on approach to RAF Hullavington.
21 January 1932	Writer and biographer Lytton Strachey died at his home, Ham Spray House, near Marlborough.
22 January 1932	Wiltshire resident, John Creasey, the world's most prolific crime writer, published his first book *Seven by Seven*.
23 January 1891	A Service of Song was held along with magic lantern show at the Mission Room in Manningford Bruce.
24 January 1928	Desmond Morris, zoologist and author of *The Naked Ape*, was born in Purton.
25 January 1753	Ruth Pierce from Potterne dropped dead in the Market Place in Devizes, after protesting her innocence before God of an accusation of lying about payment for wheat.
26 January 1813	Thomas Hussey, MP for Salisbury (1774–1813), who was described as 'one of the most upright and industrious members of the House', died.
27 January 1621	Thomas Willis, physician and 'father of neuroscience', was born in Great Bedwyn.

28 January 1547	Henry VIII died, making his nine-year-old son (with Jane Seymour of Wulfhall) King Edward VI.
29 January 1820	The country was in mourning at the death of King George III.
30 January 1961	Johnny Kidd and the Pirates appeared at the Assembly Hall, Melksham.
31 January 1889	4th Marquess of Bath chaired the first meeting of the Provisional Council of the County of Wiltshire at Devizes Assize Court.
1 February 1901	The funeral of Queen Victoria and a day of general mourning, as ordered by King Edward VII.
2 February 1854	Mary Kingsland Higgs, writer and social reformer, was born in Devizes.
3 February 1832	Revd George Crabbe, poet and rector of St James's Church, died aged seventy-seven in Trowbridge.
4 February 1941	*Pride and Prejudice*, starring Laurence Olivier and Greer Garson, showed at the Regent Cinema in Swindon.
5 February 1944	Swindon Speedway champion Martin Ashby was born in Marlborough.
6 February 1804	Joseph Priestley, theologian and scientist, who first isolated oxygen at his Bowood laboratory, died in Pennsylvania.
7 February 1877	Alfred Williams, the 'Hammerman Poet', was born in Cambria Cottage, South Marston.

8 February 1841	William Henry Fox Talbot patented his Calotype process of developing photographs.
9 February 1944	Blakehill Farm Airfield opened, later becoming home to RAF Squadrons which played a major part in the D-Day Landings.
10 February 1912	England beat Ireland 6–1 at Dalymount Park, Dublin, with Swindon Town's Harold Fleming bagging a hat-trick.
11 February 1800	Pioneering photographer William Henry Fox Talbot, who lived at Lacock Abbey, was born at Melbury House in Dorset.
12 February 1947	Salisbury City Football Club was formed from the old Salisbury City and Salisbury Corinthians Clubs, both disbanded after the Second World War.
13 February 1964	Manfred Mann played at Alex Disco Salisbury.
14 February 1961	1st Chippenham & District Canine Society dog show at the King's Head in Chippenham.
15 February 1844	Henry Addington, 1st Viscount Sidmouth, PM (1801–1804) and MP for Devizes, died.
16 February 1973	The Swinging Blue Jeans performed at Salisbury City Hall.
17 February 2011	The Help for Heroes charity took out a ninety-nine-year lease on Tedworth House, for the personal recovery and assessment centre for wounded soldiers.
18 February 1980	Cecil Beaton, designer and photographer, died at Reddish House in Broad Chalke.
19 February 1945	Dakota crashed at Beech Knoll, Stourton, after taking off from RAF Zeals killing passengers and crew.
20 February 1976	Idris Rose, communist councillor on Trowbridge UDC (1961–1974), died.
21 February 1937	Godolphin School alumna, Jilly Cooper, author of *Rivals* and *Polo*, was born.
22 February 1974	James Blunt, singer songwriter, was born in Tidworth.
23 February 1971	Melinda Messenger, former Page 3 Girl turned TV presenter, was born in Swindon.
24 February 1958	First performance of William Golding's only play, *Brass Butterfly*, at the New Theatre in Oxford. It was directed by Alastair Sim.
25 February 1852	Irish poet Thomas Moore died at his home, Sloperton Cottage, in Westbrook, Bromham.

26 February 1717	Longleat inventory showed acquisition of 'a fine clock in a japan'd case' – one of four great astronomical clocks built around 1710 by Edward Cockey of Warminster.
27 February 1990	John of Gaunt School, Trowbridge, closed after violent storms damaged roofs of the Gloucester and Wingfield buildings.
28 February 1847	William Barnes, Dorset-born poet and teacher, resident of Mere, was ordained at Salisbury Cathedral.
29 February 1824	Blondin, French tightrope walker and acrobatist who performed at Wilton Park in 1873, was born in St Omer.
1 March 1633	Revd George Herbert, poet and scholar, died at the Old Rectory in Fugglestone-cum-Bemerton near Salisbury.
2 March 1925	North Wiltshire Golf Club at Chiseldon changed its name to Swindon Golf Club to avoid confusion with NWGC at Blacklands, Calne.
3 March 1878	The poet Edward Thomas, who was often inspired by Wiltshire, was born in Lambeth.
4 March 1931	Swindon Town Supporters' Club formed. Its motto: 'To help and not to hinder.'
5 March 1918	Verney Asser, thirty-year-old Australian soldier of 2nd Training Battalion, was hanged for fatally shooting his roommate, Cpl Joseph Durkin, at Sutton Veny Camp in Salisbury.
6 March 1830	Five Wiltshire Machine Breakers were tried for arson at Wiltshire Lenten Assizes, New Sarum. Three were transported for life.
7 March 1833	Twenty-seven-year-old Isambard Kingdom Brunel appointed resident engineer to the Bristol Committee of the new Great Western Railway.
8 March 1930	Douglas Hurd, politician and Home Secretary (1985–1989), was born in Marlborough.
9 March 1912	14,000 spectators watched the Swindon Town victory in the Quarter Finals against Everton 2–1.
10 March 1498	Cardinal Thomas Wolsey was ordained priest at St Peter's Church, Marlborough.
11 March 1932	Dora Carrington, artist, committed suicide at Ham Spray House where she lived in a

menage à trois with Lytton Strachey and Ralph Partridge.

12 March 1626   John Aubrey, author of *Brief Lives* and *The Natural History of Wiltshire*, was born in Easton Pierse.

13 March 1940   The Duke of Beaufort's Hounds meet at Kington Langley.

14 March 1948   Last meeting of the GWR General Meeting, presided over by Chairman Lord Portal (1945–1948), was held, before nationalisation began.

15 March 1969   Don Rogers scored two extra-time goals for Third Division Swindon Town FC beating Arsenal 3–1 in League Cup Final at Wembley.

16 March 2006   Swindon-born British Olympic athlete, Shelley Rudman, won Silver Medal at the Winter Olympics in Skeleton Bobsleigh in a record-breaking 2mins 1.49secs.

17 March 2011   BBC Wiltshire presenter Sandy Martin died of a brain tumour aged fifty-three.

18 March 1669   Samuel Brewer, botanist and son of 'the greatest medley clothier in England', was baptised in Trowbridge.

19 March 2012   Dauntsey's School performed *Miss Saigon (Schools Edition)* at the Prince Edward Theatre in London.

20 March 2009   Trowbridge Mayor, Cllr John Knight, signed the Town Partnership agreement with Oujda, Morocco, at a Civic Dinner attended by President Monsieur Lakhdar Haddouch.

21 March 1928   HM King Amanullah and Queen Sourita (Soraya Tarzi) of Afghanistan visited the GWR Works in Swindon.

22 March 1803   Thomas Helliker hanged at Salisbury for his alleged part in the anti-machine riots and for setting fire to Littleton Mill in Semington.

23 March 1981   Shelley Rudman, British Olympic athlete, was born in Swindon.

24 March 1556   Protestant martyrs William Coberley, John Maundrel and John Spicer were burned at the stake at Fisherton near Salisbury.

25 March 1956   Dickie Valentine appeared at the Gaumont Salisbury with Tommy Whittle and his Orchestra.

26 March 1944	Halifax Bomber from station Tolthorpe, Yorkshire, which suffered engine failure over Christ Church, Bradford on Avon, brought down safely over Priory Park.
27 March 1986	GWR Swindon Works doors finally closed after 145 years of business.
28 March 1961	STD (Subscriber Trunk Dialling) system introduced in Chippenham launched by Mayor Cllr RG Archard who dialled his daughter in Birmingham.
29 March 1787	Joseph Fry, chocolate manufacturer, who was born in Sutton Benger, died in Bristol.
30 March 1839	Chartist public meeting held at the Town Hall Devizes.
31 March 1991	Arnold W. Lawrence, historian and executor of the estate of younger brother T.E. Lawrence (of Arabia), died aged ninety at No. 44 Long Street, Devizes.
1 April 2009	New Wiltshire Council unitary authority formed from NW, WW, SW and Kennet District Councils.
2 April 1951	First floodlit match at the County Ground. Swindon Town FC beat Bristol City 2–1.
3 April 1982	First Hercules left RAF Lyneham for Wideawake Airfield, Ascension Island, after Argentina invaded and occupied the Falklands Islands.
4 April 1989	BBC Wiltshire Sound launched from studios at Prospect Place in Swindon.
5 April 1588	Thomas Hobbes, philosopher and author of *Leviathan*, was born in Westport St Mary, Malmesbury.
6 April 2003	David Hempleman-Adams became the first man to ski solo and unsupported to the Geomagnetic North Pole.
7 April 1892	Arthur George Street, aka A.G. Street, countryman, writer and author of *Farmer's Glory* (1932), was born in Wilton.
8 April 1837	Lady Drummond laid the foundation stone of Holy Trinity Church in Trowbridge.
9 April 1806	Isambard Kingdom Brunel, engineer and builder of the Great Western Railway and Box Tunnel, was born in Portsmouth.

10 April 1930	South Marston-born Alfred Williams, the 'Hammerman Poet', died at Ranikhet, the house he built in South Marston.
11 April 1919	Private Hona Hape, New Zealand Maori (Pioneer) Battalion, died of sickness at Codford Camp while waiting to return home after the war.
12 April 1892	Sgt Enos Molden of the Wiltshire Police was shot dead at Corsley while attempting to arrest John Gurd for murder.
13 April 2009	Alicia Hempleman-Adams, resident of Box, became the youngest person, at the age of fifteen, to trek to the North Pole.
14 April 1974	Chippenham-born Florence May Hancock, the second female President of the TUC, who lived in Bristol, died whilst visiting her sister in Chippenham.
15 April 1919	Eglantyne Jebb, teacher at St Peter's, Marlborough, set up Save the Children with her sister, Dorothy Buxton.

16 April 1232	Ela Longspée, Countess of Salisbury, laid the foundation stone of her convent at Lacock Abbey.
17 April 1960	Eddie Cochran, American rock 'n' roll singer who crashed on Rowden Hill, Chippenham, died at St Martin's Hospital in Bath.
18 April 1957	The Platters appeared at the Gaumont in Salisbury with Ronnie Aldrich and the Squadronaires.
19 April 1938	Poet Henry Newbolt, who lived at Netherhampton House (1907–1934), died.
20 April 1206	King John granted the charter to hold weekly market and annual fair in Highworth on Feast of St Michael (29 Sept).
21 April 1834	The Great Fire of Oare. Charles Kimmer, who was later hanged for the crime, set fire to the premises of Revd Maurice Hillier Goodman.
22 April 1858	Vale of Wylye Hunt races were held between Chitterne and Codford.
23 April 2001	Two Devizes vicars blessed 5,100 northern European vines at a ceremony at a'Beckett's Vineyard, a 20-acre former fruit farm at Littleton Pannell near Devizes.
24 April 1968	The Bee Gees and an orchestra appeared at the Salisbury Odeon with Dave Dee, Dozy, Beaky, Mick and Tich.
25 April 1904	*Checkmate* by Andrew Halliday was the first production by the GWR (Swindon) Mechanics' Institute Amateur Theatrical Society.
26 April 1630	Metaphysical poet Revd George Herbert was instituted as rector of Fugglestone and Bemerton.
27 April 1932	Forty-six men on the Swindon Employment Exchange register were engaged to dig potatoes by the Jersey Farmers' Union, the first time in sixty years that non-French workers had been employed.
28 April 1653	The Great Fire of Marlborough started in a High Street tannery yard, destroying the Guildhall, St Mary's Church, County Armoury and 240 houses, inns and shops.
29 April 1968	Corsham and Derry Hill resident, composer Sir Michael Tippett, appeared on BBC's Desert Islands Discs. His favourite disc: Besse Smith 'St Louis Blues'.

30 April 1887	Harold Fleming, one of Swindon Town FC's greatest players, was born in Downton.
1 May 1672	Joseph Addison, co-founder of the *Spectator* and MP for Malmesbury, was born at the Rectory in Milston, Amesbury.
2 May 1965	The Beatles stayed at the Antrobus Arms, Amesbury, for three days while filming *Help!* on Salisbury Plain.
3 May 1839	Twenty men from 'A' Division of the Metropolitan Police were dispatched to Devizes to deal with unrest due to Chartist meetings.
4 May 1984	Swindon-born film star Diana Dors died.
5 May 1910	Swindon Town FC won the Dubonnet Cup in Paris, 2–1 against Barnsley.
6 May 1953	RAF engineer Leading Aircraftman Ronald Maddison died while participating in secret nerve gas experiments at Porton Down.
7 May 1895	The Rt Hon. Joseph Chamberlain opened new buildings and officially inaugurated Dauntsey's Agricultural School (becoming Dauntsey's School in 1930).
8 May 1858	J. Meade Falkner, author of *Moonfleet*, was born in Manningford Bruce.
9 May 1904	GWR steam locomotive the City of Truro was the first to break the 100mph speed barrier on its run from Plymouth to Bristol.
10 May 1967	Swindon-born tenor Arthur Carron, principal tenor at the Metropolitan Opera House New York and Covent Garden, died.
11 May 1965	The Kinks performed at the Odeon in Swindon, supported by The Yardbirds and Goldie & the Gingerbreads.
12 May 2010	Carol Ann Duffy held a poetry reading for the Swindon Literature Festival at STEAM Museum.
13 May 1911	Neeld Hall and Market Yard in Chippenham was opened by Hon. Lady Harriet and Lt. Col. Sir Audley Neeld.
14 May 1991	HRH Princess Diana visited Salisbury Guildhall.
15 May 1996	Swindon-born David Hempleman-Adams led the Ultimate Challenge team of novices to ski to the Magnetic North Pole.
16 May 1959	Freedom of the Borough of Swindon granted to the Wiltshire Regiment (Duke of Edinburgh's),

their last appearance before being amalgamated with the Royal Berks.

17 May 1990	The Queen visited RAF Lyneham on the fiftieth anniversary of the air base.
18 May 1940	RAF Lyneham opened Number 33 Maintenance Unit with four officers, one other rank, fifteen civilians and two vehicles, but no aircraft.
19 May 1988	Robin Tanner, etcher, printmaker, teacher and HMI of Schools for Oxfordshire, died at his home Old Chapel Field, Kington Langley.
20 May 2011	Paulo Di Canio appointed manager of Swindon Town FC.
21 May 1942	RAF Zeals opened as a forward operating airfield in Colerne sector of No. 10 Group Bomber Command.
22 May 1981	Prime Minister Margaret Thatcher opened Airfoil Ltd, a new factory of fibreglass business in Warminster, which was started by Robert Evans.
23 May 1933	A world record free-fall parachute jump achieved by Dane, John Tranum at RAF Flying Training School at Netheravon Airfield, dropping from 20,000ft and opening his parachute at 2,750 ft.
24 May 1854	2,000 visitors attended the laying of the foundation stone of the Mechanics' Institute in Swindon by Lord Methuen with Daniel Gooch, GWR Superintendent of Locomotives.
25 May 1940	First Hawker Hurricanes arrived at RAF Wroughton to be prepared by the Maintenance Unit for active service.
26 May 1874	Revd Francis Kilvert of Langley Burrell recorded an inspection by the Rural Dean: 'He said he had no fault to find and could not pick a hole in our coats. Croquet, tea and supper at Langley Green.'
27 May 1940	The War Department requisitioned the north side of the West Stand (now Town End) at Swindon Town FC for use as an air-raid shelter.
28 May 2011	Auctioneers Henry Aldridge & Son in Devizes set the world record of £220,000 for *Titanic* memorabilia, with the sale of the ship's plan (10m length) used in the official inquiry.

29 May 1660	Ancient decree proclaimed to celebrate Oak Apple Day in Great Wishford and ancient right to collect firewood from nearby Grovely Woods.
30 May 1536	Henry VIII married Jane Seymour of Wulfhall (Wolf Hall), Savernake Forest, at Whitehall Palace.
31 May 1928	Nicholas Shakespeare Hathaway of Hathaways Churn Manufactory, Old Road, Chippenham, took out a patent for an improved carpet sweeper.
1 June 1906	The Great Swindon Tram Disaster, when brake failure led to an accident resulting in five deaths and thirty injured.
2 June 1940	Chippenham Local Defence Volunteers (Home Guard) formed at a meeting in a field adjoining the Secondary School on Cocklebury Road.
3 June 1965	A UFO sighting (cigar-shaped object in sky) at Heytesbury near Warminster.
4 June 1957	The Queen and the Duke of Edinburgh's first flight in a Comet jet plane from RAF Lyneham.
5 June 2007	The Wiltshire flag with the Great Bustard symbol was accepted and raised at County Hall.

6 June 1903	Memorial plaque was unveiled at Coate House, the birthplace of Richard Jefferies the nature writer.
7 June 1761	John Rennie, engineer and surveyor to the Kennet and Avon Canal, was born.
8 June 1940	Mayor of Swindon, Cllr HR Hustings, called for 5,000 more blood donor volunteers for the Army Blood Transfusion Service.
9 June 1973	Crime writer John Creasey, of New Hall, Bodenham near Salisbury, died.

10 June 1668	Samuel Pepys visited Old Sarum and 'Stonage'.
11 June 1926	Australian opera singer Dame Nellie Melba gave her final performance in this country at the Garrison Theatre, Tidworth, before retiring.
12 June 1874	Revd Francis Kilvert of Langley Burrell recorded in his diary losing his bathing drawers in rough seas and emerging naked in front of a group of ladies while on holiday in the Isle of Wight.
13 June 1842	First railway journey by a reigning monarch, Queen Victoria, on GWR line from Slough to Paddington taking twenty-five minutes – 'Free from dust and crowd and heat, and I am quite charmed with it', she wrote the following day.
14 June 1648	'Sudden hideous and devoureinge fire' in Ramsbury destroyed goods and dwellings of 130 families, valued at £15,000.
15 June 1983	French Secretary for State for Consumer Affairs, Mme Catherine Lalumière, opened Norman Foster's Renault Building in Swindon.
16 June 1668	Lady Margaret Hungerford founded the Almshouses, Free School and Master's House in Corsham.
17 June 1990	Demonstration by Swindon residents at Faringdon Road Park about the Football League's decision to demote Swindon Town FC from First Division to Division Three because of payment irregularities to players.
18 June 1910	Visit by Lt Gen. Sir RSS Baden-Powell to review progress of the Boy Scouts movement at rally in the GWR Park in Swindon.
19 June 1215	King John signed the Magna Carta at Runnymede. One of only four original copies is held in the Chapter House at Salisbury Cathedral.
20 June 1775	Ball lightning was witnessed in a thunderstorm at Steeple Ashton.
21 June 1887	Laying of Trowbridge Town Hall foundation stone, part of Queen Victoria's Golden Jubilee celebrations.
22 June 1988	Duncan Shearer signed to Swindon Town FC from Huddersfield Town for the world record (at the time) price of £250,000.
23 June 1975	David Howell, professional golfer who has been ranked 10th in the world (2006), was born in Swindon.

24 June 1925	Visit to Swindon by members of the International Railway Congress.
25 June 1972	Acker Bilk performed at a concert in aid of the NSPCC at the Wyvern Theatre, Swindon.
26 June 1940	Luftwafffe dropped four small bombs on Boscombe Down airfield – no damage.
27 June 1948	Three RAF Lyneham York squadrons took part in the Berlin Airlift to West Berlin, whose food and supplies had been cut off by the Soviet Union.
28 June 1958	HM Queen Elizabeth and the Queen Mother visited Salisbury for the 700th anniversary of the consecration of the cathedral.
29 June 1860	The body of three-and-a-half-year-old Francis Saville Kent was found in the outside privy of Road Hill House. His half-sister, Constance Kent, later confessed to the murder.
30 June 1841	The whole length of the Great Western Railway between London and Bristol became operational with the opening of the Box Tunnel.
1 July 2011	Last Hercules flew out of RAF Lyneham, to be relocated to RAF Brize Norton.
2 July 1924	Ushers Wiltshire Brewery Ltd Centenary Celebration Excursion for employees to the Empire Exhibition at Wembley Park.
3 July 1989	(Luigi) Lou Macari, manager of Swindon TFC, resigned to join West Ham United.
4 July 2005	Heelis, the National Trust's new Headquarters in Swindon, opened its doors.
5 July 1866	Lord Shelburne, 4th Marquess of Lansdowne, MP for Calne (1856–1858) and GWR Board Chairman (1859–1863), died.
6 July 1961	Sir Charles Chitham, chairman of Wiltshire Standing Committee, laid the foundation stone for the Wiltshire police headquarters in Devizes.
7 July 1771	John Britton, antiquary and topographer, was born in Kington St Michael near Chippenham.
8 July 2012	Swindon: the Opera was performed by 250-strong local cast and crew at STEAM Museum in Swindon.
9 July 1941	*Marx Brothers Go West* was shown at the Gaumont Palace Cinema, Salisbury.
10 July 2000	*Animal Park*, with Kate Humble and Ben Fogle, and featuring Longleat Safari Park, was first shown on BBC2.

11 July 1968	Severe flooding affected Chippenham High Street and the Town Bridge.
12 July 1869	Two performances by Powell & Co.'s Circus on the Green in Devizes, with a cavalcade of horses, riders and carriages through the town.
13 July 1643	Battle of Roundway Down: the most important Royalist cavalry victory in the English Civil War led by Sir Ralph Hopton against Sir William Waller.
14 July 1974	David Mitchell, actor, comedian and writer, was born in Salisbury.
15 July 1941	RAF Keevil opened with good aircraft storage facilities later used for locally built Spitfires.
16 July 1869	Fire destroyed a factory in Mason's Lane, Bradford on Avon, which was occupied by M. Wilkins, clothier, and the property of Mr Joseph Sparks, causing £4,000 worth of damage.
17 July 2005	Former Prime Minister Sir Edward Heath died at his home in Arundells, Salisbury.
18 July 1944	Artist Rex Whistler, who lived in Salisbury as a boy and was stationed at Codford Camp, was killed in France.
19 July 2010	The Duchess of Cornwall attended the Freedom of the City of Salisbury ceremony for The Rifles (successor to the Wiltshire Regiment).
20 July 1935	The Seymour Housing Estate in Trowbridge opened.
21 July 1972	*Son et Lumière* was performed at Salisbury Cathedral, with the script by Dennis Constanduros and narrated by Michael Hordern.
22 July 1944	Rick Davies, musician and founder of Supertramp, was born in Swindon.
23 July 1962	The Wiltshire Wildlife Trust was founded by seven subscribers in response to a threat to a colony of Purple Emperor butterflies on Blackmoor Copse.
24 July 1921	Explorer Ernest Shackleton gave two lectures on his 1915–16 expedition on the Endurance at the Empire Theatre, Swindon.
25 July 1907	Cyril Luckham, TV, film and stage actor, was born in Salisbury.
26 July 1921	Ecologist geneticist and lepidopterist Philip Sheppard was born in Marlborough.

27 July 1881	Eighty Marlborough College boys (first paying passengers) travelled on the new GWR extension of the line from Swindon.
28 July 1986	Emery Gate Shopping Centre in Chippenham was opened.
29 July 1770	Convict Isaac Nichols, who became first Postmaster of New South Wales in 1809, was born in Calne.
30 July 1938	Melksham Hospital opened.
31 July 1908	The Trilithon (Stonehenge) trademark of Avon Indian Rubber Co. (Melksham) was registered, along with the phrase 'Symbols of Endurance.'
1 August 1774	Joseph Priestley's first isolation of what we now call oxygen in his 'laboratory' at Bowood House.
2 August 2004	Salisbury resident Phil Harding, *Time Team's* resident trench-excavator, opened Chiseldon Museum.
3 August 1858	John Hanning Speke, explorer, who died in a shooting accident at Neston Park, discovered Lake Victoria, the source of the Nile.
4 August 1914	At 7.49 a.m. ten blasts of the GWR Works hooter signalled the start of the First World War.
5 August 1905	General William Booth, founder of the Salvation Army, visited Swindon.
6 August 1858	Netheravon beat Vale of Wylye Cricket Club in a match held at Stonehenge.
7 August 1985	Roger Moore, along with Patrick McKnee, was on location at the Renault Building Swindon for James Bond film, *A View to a Kill.*
8 August 1990	The Queen reopened the restored Kennet & Avon Canal.
9 August 1932	Funeral of Mr H.G. Harris, the 2nd son and last survivor of Thomas Harris, founder of Messrs C. & T. Harris (Calne) Ltd. He died after falling in the chill room at the factory.
10 August 1891	During a thunderstorm at Overton near Marlborough, forty-seven sheep were killed by lightning.
11 August 2012	Ed McKeever from Bradford on Avon won an Olympic Gold Medal in the 200m kayak sprint at Eton Dorney.
12 August 1891	Bazaar held at Edington Monastery Gardens in aid of the church.

13 August 1912	Octavia Hill, social reformer and one of the founders of the National Trust, died.
14 August 1936	Actor Trevor Bannister, who played Mr Lucas in *Are You Being Served?*, was born in Durrington.
15 August 1966	The Great Fire of Melksham destroyed the Finished Goods store, part of the Avon Rubber Co., with £1 million worth of damage.
16 August 1986	Centenary Celebration Dinner for Walter Goodall George's World Record Mile Race held at Calne John Bentley School. Guests included world record-breaking runners Christopher Brasher, Sydney Wooderson and Derek Ibbotson.
17 August 1912	Central Flying School, part of the new Royal Flying Corps, opened at RAF Upavon.
18 August 2011	The 167th and last repatriation of bodies of service personnel passed through Wootton Bassett from RAF Lyneham en route to John Radcliffe Hospital, Oxford.
19 August 1833	The title 'Great Western Railway' was adopted at meeting of the London and Bristol Committees.
20 August 1912	General William Booth, founder of the Salvation Army, who visited Swindon in 1904, died.
21 August 1965	The Animals played at Salisbury City Hall, with support from The Mob.
22 August 1832	200 people attended a public dinner in Chippenham town centre to celebrate 'The Triumph of Reform' (The Great Reform Act increased Britain's voters from 6 per cent to 12 per cent of the population).
23 August 1886	Calne-born athlete Walter Goodall George ran the mile in 4mins 12.75secs, an unbroken record until 1931.
24 August 1687	Michael Wise, composer and organist at Salisbury Cathedral, died after a blow to the head by the nightwatch after a violent disturbance.
25 August 1869	Keevil District Horticultural Society exhibition was held with kind permission of RP Long Esq. in Rood Ashton Park.
26 August 1833	Henry Fawcett, the first blind MP, economist and campaigner for women's rights, was born in Salisbury.

27 August 2005	Edington Festival of Music within the Liturgy celebrated its fiftieth anniversary; its theme, the 'Discipleship and the Kingdom of God'.
28 August 1906	Sir John Betjeman, poet laureate and pupil at Marlborough College (1920–1925), was born.
29 August 1907	Messrs F. Skurray & Son, Town Flour Mills, Swindon, succeeded in competition in obtaining an order for 200 sacks of specially prepared flour for biscuit making, for South Africa.
30 August 1872	Francis Kilvert recorded the arrival of the 13th Hussars in Chippenham on their way up to Colchester from Dartmoor, where they had been on 'disastrous manoeuvres'.
31 August 1835	The Great Western Railway was created by Act of Parliament to provide double tracked line from Bristol to London (even though work had started in 1832)
1 September 1967	Poet Siegfried Sassoon died at Heytesbury.
2 September 1986	C. & T. Harris (Calne) Ltd's bacon factory was demolished.

3 September 1914	Alfred Williams resigned from his job as hammerman at GWR Works to concentrate on completing *Life in a Railway Factory*, published October 1915.
4 September 925	Coronation of Æthelstan of Malmesbury, King of Mercia and Wessex, at Kingston upon Thames.
5 September 1927	Commonweal School, Swindon, was officially opened.
6 September 1948	Chippenham-born Florence Hancock CBE became President of the TUC, receiving her ceremonial handbell at the Margate Congress.
7 September 1971	Wyvern Theatre, Swindon, was opened by the Queen and Prince Philip.
8 September 1966	Georgie Fame and The Blue Flames played at Salisbury City Hall.
9 September 1858	Walter Goodall George, athlete and record-breaking mile runner, was born in Calne.
10 September 1810	Celebration of the opening of the Wiltshire and Berkshire Canal into the River Thames at Abingdon.
11 September 1291	Queen Eleanor of Provence, wife of Henry III and mother of Edward I (Longshanks), was buried somewhere in the abbey church of St Mary's and St Melor, Amesbury.
12 September 1850	The Grand Opening of Neeld Hall and Great Cheese Market on Chippenham High Street.
13 September 1840	Daniel Gooch, GWR Superintendent of Locomotives, wrote to Brunel, Chief Engineer, proposing the building of the GWR engine works in Swindon.
14 September 1939	In the expansion of RAF Yatesbury in preparation for war, No. 10 Elementary Flying Training School was formed.
15 September 1859	Isambard Kingdom Brunel, pioneering railway engineer, died and was buried in Kensal Green Cemetery.
16 September 1929	'The first true full-length talkie', *Bulldog Drummond* starring Ronald Coleman, was shown at the Regent Cinema in Swindon. 1,800 people tried to get in to the 1,300-seat cinema.
17 September 1954	Faber and Faber published *Lord of the Flies* by William Golding, teacher at Bishop Wordsworth's School, Salisbury.

18 September 1955	Johnny Dankworth and his orchestra, along with Cleo Laine and Dennis Lotis, performed at the Gaumont in Salisbury.
19 September 1940	Heinkel bomber dropped an incendiary on an RAF Lyneham hangar, killing four civilians.
20 September 2011	The UK's first commercial hydrogen filling station opened in Swindon at Honda's South Marston plant.
21 September 1915	Mr Cecil Chubb of Bemerton Lodge, Salisbury, bought Lot 15: Stonehenge with 30 acres, for £6,600 at auction at the Palace Theatre, Salisbury.

STONEHENGE FROM THE NORTH. (*From "Our Own Country."*)

22 September 1982	Billie Piper, actress and singer, was born in Swindon.
23 September 1840	Henry Fox Talbot's first exposure of paper treated with silver oxide to light to produce a photographic negative at his home, Lacock Abbey.
24 September 1762	William Bowles, poet and vicar of Bremhill (1804–1850), was born in Northants.
25 September 1909	Swindon Boro' Military Prize Band won the National Military Band Championship at Crystal Palace, under conductor Mr F.G. Davis.
26 September 1914	Released Beirut hostage, Jackie Mann, resident in Lebanon for forty years, landed at RAF Lyneham.
27 September 1884	Another of the 'Dynamite Outrages' bomb explosions in Salisbury Market Place severely damaged the Guildhall.
28 September 1932	Opening of the new Trowbridge High School for Girls by Miss S.M. Fry JP, the first secondary school built in the county for girls only.
29 September 1999	The Devizes Millennium White Horse was completed.
30 September 1874	First Trowbridge Water Co. water was turned on by the wife of Mr R.P. Long.
1 October 1890	Avon India Rubber Co. Ltd began business in Melksham with twenty men and four women, achieving a profit of £496 18s 4d in the first year.
2 October 1835	Melksham Poor Law Union (renamed Trowbridge and Melksham in 1898) came into existence followed by the establishment of the workhouse at Semington in 1838.
3 October 1979	PC Desmond Kellam died while investigating a burglary in Church Walk, Trowbridge. He was struck with a billhook by David Octavius James, who was cleared of murder and sentenced to eight years for manslaughter.
4 October 1916	Yarnbury (Winterbourne Stoke) Sheep Fair, once one of the most important in the South West, was closed when the army commandeered the surrounding area for troop training.
5 October 1594	As a result of a long-standing feud between two families, Sir Henry Long was killed by

Sir Henry Danvers (later Earl of Danby) and his brother, along with other followers, whilst dining in Corsham.

6 October 1938   The first naval flying training course was held at the military flying school RAF camp Yatesbury.

7 October 2011   Inspector Wexford actor, George Baker MBE, died in West Lavington, his home for over twenty years.

8 October 1985   W.E. Chivers, Devizes building company which built the first nuclear reactor at Harwell, Oxfordshire, and Princess Margaret Hospital, Swindon, went into receivership.

9 October 2005   Actress Shirley Eaton, who was sprayed gold in *Goldfinger*, attended book signing of *James Bond Girls* at Infinitely Better in Brunel Centre, Swindon.

10 October 1923   Opening of the new Trowbridge Town Football Club grandstand at Bythesea Road ground (now the site of County Hall).

11 October 1886   Thomas Hardy attended the funeral of William Barnes, Dorset-born poet and philologist, who lived and taught in Mere (1823–1835) and died in Winterborne Came.

12 October 1974   Stephen Lee, professional snooker player, was born in Trowbridge.

13 October 1915   Marlborough College alumnus, poet Charles Hamilton Sorley, died at the Battle of Loos in France aged twenty.

14 October 1946   Justin Hayward, singer songwriter with The Moody Blues, was born in Swindon.

15 October 1889   Sir Daniel Gooch, GWR engineer (1837–1864) and Chairman (1865–1889), died aged seventy-three.

16 October 2011   Wootton Bassett was granted Royal status at a ceremony attended by the Princess Royal (only the third UK town and the 1st in over 100 years).

17 October 1961   Mrs Hilary Robinson of Schauffer, The Ley, Box, was sworn in as 1st Female Special Constable in Wiltshire.

18 October 2008   World-record price of £94,000 was paid for *Titanic* memorabilia at Henry Aldridge & Son, Devizes, for First-Class Steward Edmund Stone's pocket watch.

19 October 1858	30,000 £10 shares were on offer for Berks & Hants Railway Extension to GWR.
20 October 1636	Sir Christopher Wren, architect of St Paul's Cathedral, was born in East Knoyle.
21 October 1839	Chitterne Stone commemorates Farmer Dean of Imber who was attacked and defended himself against four highway robbers on the Lavington Road.
22 October 1981	Clarendon Upper School in Trowbridge performed Offenbach's *Orpheus in the Underworld*.
23 October 1931	Actress Diana Dors was born in Swindon.
24 October 1537	Jane Seymour, the 3rd wife of Henry VIII, whose family seat was Wulfhall, Savernake Forest, died after giving birth to Prince Edward, the future King Edward VI.
25 October 1840	GWR's first recorded accident at Faringdon Road Engine Shed.
26 October 1918	Sir Cecil Chubb of Bemerton Lodge, near Salisbury, owner of Stonehenge, handed it over to Sir Alfred Mond, first Commissioner of Works, as a gift to the Nation.
27 October 939	Æthelstan, first King of a united England, died in Malmesbury.
28 October 2008	Archbishop of Canterbury consecrated Salisbury Cathedral's first new permanent font (bronze on Purbeck stone base) by artist William Pye.
29 October 2003	David Hempleman-Adams became the first person to fly a balloon solo with an open wicker basket across the Atlantic from Canada to the UK.
30 October 1918	Funeral of Edwin Giddings, wine and spirit merchant, at St John's Church in Devizes.
31 October 2007	The Wiltshire and Swindon History Centre opened in Cocklebury Road, Chippenham.
1 November 1943	Residents of Imber were given forty-seven days' notice to evacuate their homes as the village became the training area for American troops for the D-Day landings.
2 November 1827	Irish poet Thomas Moore, who lived near Bromham, recorded in his diary visiting Bowood, where his friend Lord Lansdowne had just received news of his appointment to Lord Lieutenant of the county.

3 November 1810	'Cheap travelling by the old Salisbury coach from the Black Horse, Salisbury; the Bell and Crown Inn, Holborn; and the Saracen's Head, Friday-st every afternoon. Inside fare 16s. Outside 10s 6d.'
4 November 1816	A lioness escaped from a travelling menagerie parked at The Pheasant Inn, Winterslow, and was later recaptured by owners.
5 November 1663	Elizabeth Godolphin, benefactor and founder of the Godolphin School in Salisbury, was baptised at St Thomas à Becket, Coulston near Westbury. She died in 1726 and is buried with her husband, Charles, and family in the west cloister of Westminster Abbey.
6 November 1848	Richard Jefferies, nature writer (*Red Deer*, *Bevis, the Story of a Boy* and *Wood Magic*, a *Fable*), was born in Coate near Swindon.
7 November 1943	Training began at 101st (Airborne Division) Parachute Jump School in the grounds of the 502nd Battalion area at Chilton Foliat Camp.
8 November 1968	'Frank! Fascinating!' First showing of *Helga*, the first sex education film, certificate 'A' at ABC Cinema, Swindon.

9 November 1949	Elise and Doris Walters, comedy duo Gert and Daisy, appeared at the Empire Swindon.
10 November 1895	The Hon. Mrs Victor Bruce (Mildred Petrie), aviatrix, racing motorist, businesswomen and resident of Bradford on Avon, was born.

11 November 2000	BBC Radio Swindon launched separately from BBC Radio Wiltshire.
12 November 1937	Closing down sale of Hathaways Ltd, Chippenham, which produced world famous butter churns and 'The World's Best Carpet Sweeper'.

13 November 1820	Gypsy Edward Buckland murdered widow Judith Pearce from Seagry.
14 November 1872	*The Times* published a long and controversial letter by Richard Jefferies on the lives of Wiltshire agricultural labourers.
15 November 1950	Princess Elizabeth visited Swindon to open the new Garden of Remembrance on Groundwell Road, and toured the BR Works, officially naming steam locomotive No. 7037 'Princess Elizabeth', the last one of the famous Castle class.
16 November 1926	Arthur Samuel Spencer and John Leslie George opened Arthur Spencer & Co., music warehouse and seller of gramophone records and radios, at No. 45 Fore Street, Trowbridge (a Grade 1 listed building, now HSBC).
17 November 1902	A Choral Festival was held at Primitive Methodist Church, Chippenham, with selections from Haydn's *Creation*.
18 November 1924	Messrs J.C. & C.A. Plaister engaged twenty chess players in an exhibition of simultaneous play at Swindon GWR's Mechanics' Institute: eleven wins, five draws and four losses.

19 November 1991	Released Beirut hostage, Terry Waite, arrived at RAF Lyneham.
20 November 1993	Memorial service for Nobel Prize winning author William Golding at Salisbury Cathedral.
21 November 1843	Thomas Hancock, inventor and father of the rubber industry, was born in Marlborough.
22 November 1910	First Royal Aero Club Flying Certificate issued at Larkhill airfield to J.J. Hammond.
23 November 1937	T.C. Usher, Chairman of Usher's Wiltshire Brewery, launched the newly installed bottling plant in Trowbridge.
24 November 1983	Dean Ashton, former West Ham and English striker, was born in Swindon.
25 November 1985	Poet Geoffrey Grigson died at home in Broad Town.
26 November 1967	The Hercules Fleet was involved in Operation Jacobin, airlifting service personnel from the Gulf of Aden.
27 November 1943	Bernie Wright and Phyllis Daniels were the last couple to marry at St Giles's Church, Imber, before the evacuation of the village by the War Office.
28 November 2008	John Lawrence, aka Lord Oaksey, former jockey, and horse racing journalist, received the Peter O'Sullivan Award for Services to Racing.
29 November 1879	First recorded match of Swindon Town Football Club (originally called Swindon Association Football Club).
30 November 1978	Salisbury Playhouse opened by Sir Alec Guinness.
1 December 1938	No. 2 Electrical & Wireless School for training radio operators opened at RAF Yatesbury camp.
2 December 1740	Bratton schoolmaster Thomas Whitaker's diary recorded bad weather in the evening: 'Several persons struck down by thunder and lightning.'
3 December 1967	The world's first heart transplant by Dr Christiaan Barnard, using components made by Vickers of South Marston.
4 December 1679	Thomas Hobbes of Malmesbury, philosopher, author of *Leviathan*, died at Hardwick Hall, Derbyshire, home of the Cavendish family.
5 December 1839	Commander Samuel Meredith was confirmed as the first Chief Constable of Wiltshire Constabulary.

6 December 1872	Revd Francis Kilvert of Langley Burrell dined with the Dallins at Langley Lodge: 'A handsome and most hospitable entertainment and a very friendly evening, two soups, champagne and curaçao.'
7 December 1983	William Golding gave his Nobel Prize for Literature acceptance speech at award ceremony in Sweden.
8 December 1730	Jan Ingen Housz, Dutch physiologist, biologist and chemist, was born in Breda. He discovered photosynthesis and is buried at St Mary's Church, Calne.
9 December 2011	The Princess Royal opened the new £4 million Dents glove factory in Furnax Lane, Warminster.
10 December 1881	Walter Powell, MP for Malmesbury, philanthropist and balloonist, was lost at sea when his balloon, Saladin, came down in the English Channel.
11 December 1783	Sarah Jarvis died aged 107. Her memorial at St Bartholomew's Church, Corsham, states 'Sometime before her death she had fresh teeth'.
12 December 1817	Devizes Saving Bank was established.
13 December 1918	Westbury MP Masseh Lopes sentenced to two years and fined £10,000 for election bribery.
14 December 1940	No. 2 Air Observer Navigation School (AONS) RAF Yatesbury closed down having trained 247 pupils.
15 December 1891	The Trowbridge Cattle Show annual dinner was held at the George Hotel.
16 December 1965	Manfred Mann performed at Salisbury City Hall.
17 December 2012	The RAF Ensign was symbolically lowered for the last time at RAF Lyneham before becoming a Defence Technical Training College.
18 December 1657	Sir Edward Bayntun of Battle House, Bromham, MP for Devizes and High Sheriff of Wiltshire, died.
19 December 1933	George Jackson Churchward, CBE, JP, Chief Mechanical Engineer GWR Co, 1st Mayor, 1st Hon. Freeman of Borough of Swindon, died aged seventy-six years.
20 December 1854	Special rally with entertainment, in aid of the Patriotic Fund for sick and wounded of the

	Crimean War, held at the Mechanics' Institute Swindon.
21 December 1971	Led Zeppelin played at Salisbury City Hall.
22 December 1971	English section of the M4 between J9 &15 (Maidenhead to Swindon) opened.
23 December 2011	The 7-millionth book was transferred from Oxford University's Bodleian Library to its new overflow storage facility in South Marston, Swindon.
24 December 1968	The Coronation Car Sales, Victoria Road, Swindon, 'Yuletide Gesture. You'll find a free turkey in the boot of all cars purchased until Christmas Eve.'
25 December 1965	Carol Service at Salisbury Cathedral led by UK vocal harmony trio The Ivy League (who had two Top Ten hit singles that year).
26 December 1833	Isambard Kingdom Brunel was appointed Chief Engineer to the Great Western Railway.
27 December 1830	Wiltshire Machine Breakers tried at Special Commission Assizes in New Sarum.
28 December 1809	The Kennet & Avon Canal was completed and opened.
29 December 1922	GWR Excursions to Newbury Steeplechases.
30 December 1940	The High Altitude Flight Unit was created at Boscombe Down airfield, to investigate aircraft operation at 30,000-plus feet.
31 December 1925	Daphne Oram, sound engineer and composer, and founder of the BBC Radiophonic Workshop, was born at Ivy House in Devizes.

BIBLIOGRAPHY

BOOKS

Aubrey, John, *The Natural History of Wiltshire*

Berryman, Dave, *Wiltshire Airfields in the Second World War*

Defoe, Daniel, *A Tour through the Whole of Great Britain (1724 1726)*

Hatchwell, Richard, *Art in Wiltshire*

Pepys, Samuel, *The Diary of Samuel Pepys (1660–1669)*

Plomer, William, *Kilvert's Diary 1870-1879: Selections from the Diary of the Rev. Francis Kilvert*

Simple, Paul, *The Oldest and the Best, The History of the Wiltshire Constabulary 1839–2003*

Woodruffe, Brian J., *Parish Churches of Wiltshire: A Guide*

OTHER

William Cobbett's *Rural Rides* (1830) (www.visionofbritain.org.uk)

The Victoria History of the County of Wiltshire

Kelly's and Pigot's Directories

Pevsner's *Wiltshire*

The Swindon Society, *A Century of Swindon*

Graham Carter's 'Chronicle of Swindon' from the *Swindon Advertiser*

WEBSITES

www.alfredwilliams.org.uk

www.bbc.co.uk

www.britishnewspaperarchive.co.uk

www.britishlistedbuildings.co.uk

www.history.wiltshire.gov.uk/community
www.historyofparliamentonline.org
www.gov.uk/defence–infrastructure (MOD)
www.greatwestern.org.uk
www.imdb.com
www.oxforddnb.com (Oxford Dictionary of National Biography)
www.salisburycathedral.org.uk/
www.south–central–media.co.uk
www.swindonweb.com
www.thisiswiltshire.co.uk/news
www.whbt.org.uk (Wiltshire Historic Buildings Trust)

National Archives currency converter was used for equivalent 2005 spending value of yesterday's money.

ILLUSTRATIONS

Thanks to Simon Drew for Hengehogs; Gary Dawes for the Acrebury logo; Frances Alexander for Sweet Roman Hand italic script; Graham Lamat for the crop circle digital drawings, and lightunderthebushel for use of the Great Bustard Morris logo.

Also to Mike Prior and Helen Pocock for use of their Wiltshire Flag design; the landlord of The Moonrakers, Pewsey, for his pub sign image; Dents Warminster for glove adverts; Bradford on Avon Museum for Royal Enfield advert; Athelstan Museum for Flying Monk pub sign and Thomas Hobbes images; Gill Hutchinson for use of Roger Hutchinson's Stonehenge Free Festival Poster, and Box Steam Brewery for their logo.

Other illustrations are courtesy of the Calne Heritage Centre, Chippenham Museum, Swindon Library and WHSC. The sketch of William Golding is by the author. Other images from author photos digitised by Alfred La Vardera. All other images, including *Punch* cartoons, are out of copyright as far as it has been possible to establish.